Best wishes to Noel
and B...

GW00759545

Trade for the People

Trade
for the
People

Frank Bamford

The Book Guild Ltd
Sussex, England

To Dorothy, who has endured for many years my obsession with this subject but who shares my concern for all the people who, in the interests of trade, have laboured so long for so little, and have often been denied the opportunity to labour. To them also this book is dedicated.

The Book Guild Limited
Temple House
25 High Street
Lewes, Sussex

First published 1990
© Frank Bamford 1990

Set in Baskerville

Typesetting by Book Economy Services
Burgess Hill

Printed in Great Britain by
Antony Rowe Ltd
Chippenham

British Library Cataloguing in Publication Data
Bamford, Frank W. (Frank Wallace)
    Trade for the people
    1. Great Britain. Economic conditions, history
    I. Title
    330.941

ISBN 0 86332 525 4

Contents

List of Diagrams

Foreword

by Sir Donald MacDougall

Anyone who finds Britain's present large trade deficit, and other aspects of the economy, disturbing, and the outlook worrying, will find much food for thought in this essay by Frank Bamford on 'Trade for the People'. In an historical perspective it analyses developments, particularly, but no means wholly, in the field of foreign trade, leading up to our current predicaments. The author takes us back a couple of centuries, although about half the book concerns the last twenty years.

He writes in a clear, highly readable, style which he modestly described to me as 'pop economics' but which I regard as in many respects economics as it should be written by far more economists nowadays. It is understandable to the layman, without any mathematical symbols – or even footnotes. There is, however, an Appendix describing the many published sources on which he has drawn in addition to his own rich and varied experience as a student of economics and economic history, a civil servant and finally, for many years, a business-man, during which period a company in whose export sales effort he was playing a leading part, won the Queen's Award for Exports.

The author pulls no punches, and if he has found it necessary to mention some unfashionable, controversial and even what may seem to some readers outrageous, ideas, this only goes to show how deep a hole we are in. Although I have doubts about some of his proposed remedies for our economic ills, this in no way detracts from the value of his stimulating analysis. This book deserves to be widely read.

October 1989

7

Introduction

When I studied economics and modern economic history at the London School of Economics in the late 1940s, I became especially interested in the major economic developments in the nineteenth and twentieth centuries which had determined the condition of the people of Britain. The extent to which these developments related to our overseas trading position became increasingly revealed to me, as were the startling changes which had occurred in this position over 150 years.

After some fifteen years in and around Westminster, I subsequently became heavily involved in the export drive and specifically in developing overseas nuclear fuel businesses. My colleagues and I experienced the triumph of a Queen's Award for Exports followed swiftly by the disaster of the 1979–82 period. For the last five years I have run my own small company which has been engaged in mineral and other ventures in Africa and Europe, thus extending my international perspective even further.

Throughout this long experience, my interest in the subjects I read at LSE has never been deeply buried. During the last few years the obscurantism and lack of realism in the fashionable discussion of economic affairs, coupled with the deep seriousness of the underlying position of the UK, have led me to relate recent developments to the conditioning history of the last two centuries. Now, at last, it seems that realism is beginning to break through into a public consciousness that something is badly wrong which can no longer be obscured by propaganda masquerading as information. So it may well be timely for fresh voices to be heard to contribute to current debate about what has gone wrong and what has to be done to put it right.

This is the task I have set myself in writing this essay, which, with a brevity which is no doubt breath-taking, sketches the economic history of our country since Napoleon as a preface to more detailed discussion of the post-war years and especially the last decade. Throughout it emphasises the vital importance of Britain's international trading position and its impact on the condition of the people.

My general theme is that Britain has never been a great exporter of manufactured goods since the textile and railways bonanza of the mid nineteenth century, and for specific historical and social reasons has always lagged behind other major countries in applying herself to the sophisticated requirements of modern industry.

For some decades after the Second World War, substantial although uneven progress was made in achieving export goals, but the country's undue exposure to overseas trade problems continuously led to the application of deflationary brakes on consumption and investment so that industry never developed with confidence into the sustained growth which could have constituted the basis for successfully resolving the country's major economic problems including inflation. When a fair degree of recovery had been achieved from particularly devastating afflictions in the 1970s, the policies of 1979–1983 so damaged manufacturing industry that we now face the most serious crisis of all amidst continuing high unemployment. Some remedies are proposed particularly to reverse crippling import penetrations.

The book is directed to the intelligent non-specialist. So technical economic terms, jargon, detailed references and footnotes are avoided as far as possible. A few key terms are however unavoidable and the following glossary explains these briefly. Appendix III contains an account of the principal sources which have been drawn upon.

I must record my great appreciation for the notable assistance given to me by Sir Donald MacDougall with whom I entered into correspondence somewhat by accident. He has made numerous helpful comments on my first and later drafts, saving me from some serious errors and making many positive suggestions. The remaining errors and omissions are entirely my own responsibility.

POSTSCRIPT – UPDATE TO 1990

This book, including the above Introduction, was completed in September 1989. Now, in the early days of 1990, it is interesting to consider how the most recent developments relate to the book's thesis.

Most notably, the Chancellor of the Exchequer has resigned on the grounds of a policy disagreement with the Prime Minister. However, such an event can hardly be regarded as the celebration of successful policies but rather as a bitter dispute as to which escape route to attempt out of a deep morass.

In the event, sterling has been allowed to fall further to a level over 11% lower than a year ago. Thus part of a necessary condition for recovery has been established, albeit by passivity in the face of the economically and politically uncceptable alternative of even higher interest rates.

The near-stagnation of the economy inevitably continued into 1990 with inflation nevertheless still obstinately high. The 'Invisible' trade surplus continued its descent to an almost negligible level and despite a modest improvement in 'Visible' trade the total Current Balance was still running at an annual rate of £20 billion in the three months to November. It is clearly going to take a long period of stagnation to correct these grave symptoms of disorder, with little prospect of a firm basis for sustained economic expansion.

Central to the governmental policy dispute is the question of Britain's attitude to the consolidation of the European Community, particularly to the E.M.S. Debate on this issue has intensified in recent months with the Prime Minister arguing that the first requirement is the completion of a single market involving the free movement of capital in respect of which Britain 'leads' other countries. Particularly noteworthy is the openness of British companies to takeovers by foreigners. Recently, Jaguar has been taken over by Ford, and Morgan Grenfell by the Deutsche Bank which already controls many German industrial companies.

The idea of progress by takeover has been identified as a peculiarly Anglo-Saxon concept breeding short-term outlooks quite inconsistent with the wider and longer term responsibilities of management, embracing the interests of employees as well as shareholders, in countries where hostile takeovers are extremely difficult. In Germany, industrialists, workpeople, bankers and governments have together achieved a level of manufacturing production and exports almost 2½ times as great as Britain's. Rather than seeking to change this successful business culture in favour of freer markets, moving

11

more into line with it looks like one right direction in which to guide Trade for the People.

January 1990

Glossary

GDP. Gross Domestic Product, the accepted measure of the country's total output.

EMS. European Monetary System, the agreement linking the currencies of most of the European community countries into a pattern of exchange rates allowing only small variations except by prior agreement which has occasionally been given.

Visible Exports and Imports. Trade in goods which can be physically identified such as food, basic materials and manufactured goods.

Invisible Exports and Imports. Trade in services, such as tourism, transport and financial services, as well as income from investments and transfer payments especially to and from the European Community.

Balance of Trade. Balance of Visible Exports and Imports

Balance of Payments. Balance of both Visible and Invisible Trade taken together, i.e. the Current Account of the Balance of Payments.

Terms of Trade. This is an index of the ratio of average export prices to average import prices expressed in relation to a base year when the index is 100. A figure of more than 100 in a later year is regarded as 'favourable' in that export prices increased in relation to import prices, indicating that fewer goods needed to be exported to pay for the same volume of imports; and vice versa for an 'unfavourable' movement of the index.

I

After Napoleon

'By the adoption of one machine in particular, one man performed the work of many, and the superfluous labourers were thrown out of employment and left to starve. Yet it is to be observed, that the work thus executed was inferior in quality, not marketable at home, and merely hurried over with a view to exportation. It was called in the cant of the trade, by the name of "Spider-work". The rejected workmen, in the blindness of their ignorance, instead of rejoicing at these improvements in arts so beneficial to mankind, conceived themselves to be sacrificed to improvements in mechanism. In the foolishness of their hearts they imagined that the maintenance and well-doing of the industrious poor were objects of greater consequence than the enrichment of a few individuals by any improvement in the implements of trade which threw the workmen out of employment and rendered the labourer unworthy of his hire'.

LORD BYRON in his speech in the House of Lords on the Luddite question, 27 February 1812.

The long-drawn out struggle against Napoleon and his eventual defeat marked one of the great turning points in history. For one thing, in 1815 the aggressiveness of France came to an end and with it the martial and colonial rivalry with England which had distracted Europe and much of the world for many years. Peace in Europe was established until the newly emergent German nation sought a wider hegemony, so Britain enjoyed virtually unbroken peace for a hundred years. In the twentieth century this seems almost unbelievable to the extent that with Germany finally defeated we perhaps too easily believed in a threat from a new enemy as if we were so used to war that, with suicidal weapons at our disposal, we have had to believe in our own destruction, one way or another.

But if the nineteenth century was different in that it offered a clear field for economic forces to work themselves out more in less in peace without the distraction, destruction or indeed stimulus of war, this field turned out to be scene for internal rather than international struggle. The class war brought bitter strife and suffering enough. On the political side, it is vital to recall that Napoleon emerged from the French Revolution

13

which gave English people all kinds of disturbing ideas – like democracy – disturbing certainly to the governing classes who outlawed Tom Paine and trade unions, as well as hanging the Luddites for breaking some of the new looms for weaving cloth. Fraudulently weaving in fact but that seems a mere detail to the modern economists, business men and politicians who use Luddite as a term of abuse. I wish I were able to send to every one of them the text of Byron's speech to the House of Lords on the subject.

The Napoleonic War period was one of economic turmoil as well as political awakening. The war was not only costly in itself but it also disrupted trade and caused food shortages such that the price of wheat rose astronomically at times. The modern reader may think it curious that the price of wheat is such a touchstone of relative hardship or prosperity in the

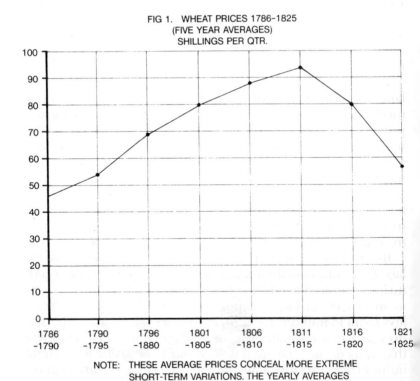

FIG 1.   WHEAT PRICES 1786–1825
(FIVE YEAR AVERAGES)
SHILLINGS PER QTR.

NOTE: THESE AVERAGE PRICES CONCEAL MORE EXTREME
SHORT-TERM VARIATIONS. THE YEARLY AVERAGES
FOR –   1800   1801   1810   1812
WERE –   113s   119s   106s   126s

early nineteenth century. When people were desperately poor, as most of them were at that time, they spent a high proportion of their income on food and a large amount of that depended on wheat and other cereals, with hardly any meat eaten by the mass of the people. It is most revealing in fact that when a little prosperity arrived, later in the century, it can be measured by a small reduction in wheat consumption per head and a significant increase in purchases of tea and sugar. Such was wealth in Victorian England.

But this is to anticipate a great deal. We must return to the early years of the century and the Luddites. During the latter part of the eighteenth century the pace of mechanical invention in the textile industry quickened remarkably. First spinning and later weaving, with cotton ahead of wool, passed from hand operation, mainly in people's houses in the villages and small towns, to workshops and factories where the new machines were assembled by the moneyed classes. The machines were driven first by water wheels, a fact which drew the new factories particularly to the flanks of the Pennines, and later by steam. So coal became vital.

During the same period the progressive enclosure of farm land enabled more economic units to replace the strips formerly cultivated by individual villagers who were often in the process deprived of their grazing rights. Many people who had previously scratched together a bare subsistence on land to which their legal rights were obscure were left without the means to feed themselves either by cultivation or by earning a pittance by hand-spinning and weaving. So a labour supply for the new factories was steadily becoming available, not only from the ranks of the impoverished hand-workers, but also from those dispossessed of land and grazing rights.

But there was more to the increase in the supply of new labour for industry than the agricultural revolution. After centuries of quite slow growth the population of England began to take off in the late eighteenth century. Around 1800 it was less than 10 million rising to some 14 million by 1825 and over 20 million by mid-century. It is important to recognise that the rate of increase accelerated in advance of the main industrial revolution. The highest rate seems to have been in the period 1810–1820, falling somewhat to mid-century. It is not important for our present purpose to analyse the reasons for this astonishing phenomenon, but it was probably mainly the result of some improvements in water supply, sanitation and midwifery causing a major reduction in infant mortality. The ordinary people did not suddenly become more fertile – most women bore many children in the eighteenth century – but, until the later years, most of the children died in infancy. In this situation it only required modest improvements in conditions to result in an explosive and cumulative growth in population.

There were in fact no dramatic changes in the lives of the ordinary people in the eighteenth century, and it would be wrong to overstate the quality of life when most people's incomes barely supported subsistence, with bad harvests causing near-famine conditions. At such times it paid merchants to import wheat from the continent and in good years they could export some from England. But for a century or two the most important and growing trade had been in woollen textiles capitalising on England's principal raw material – the wool of sheep. Even so, foreign trade was of small importance in the economic life of the country, interesting as it was for some particular areas. Imports (or exports) accounted for less than 10% of the national product.

Inevitably, as the population grew the need for improved food supplies became imperative. To a modest extent this need was met by the more productive home agriculture made possible by the enclosure movement and stimulated by the high wheat prices of the Napoleonic War years, but before long the need for greater imports led to the clamour for the removal of the import restrictions of the Corn Laws.

Textile production capacity was growing quickly and exports began to be important in cotton as well as wool. The woollen trade in 1780 had been an order of magnitude more important than cotton. The really interesting development was that the cotton trade was already growing apace by the turn of the century, propelled by the new inventions in spinning and weaving, and with the increasing incentives of the export trade. By 1820, the cotton trade was already twice as important as wool which itself had increased by 50% in forty years, and all raw cotton had to be imported.

One thing was for sure. There was no shortage of labour for the manufacture of cotton or woollen goods or indeed for the other trades galloping ahead in their wake, such as iron and steel. The scene was set for the almost incredible story of the mid-century. The industrial and commercial development which had taken place by 1815 was as nothing to what was to come.

Before we proceed, however, we should ponder further on the condition of the people at this outset of our story. We have already observed that a bare subsistence was the limit of aspiration of the vast majority of the people. The modern expectation of continuous economic progress makes it somewhat difficult to comprehend the reality of an era when such an expectation just did not exist. Indeed there is ample evidence that over the whole of the eighteenth century there had been little improvement in the lot of the common man. In fact, a slow increase in real wages up to the middle of the century seems to have been largely cancelled by a subsequent deterioration, culminating in the devastation and disruption of the Napoleonic Wars. One consequence was that the increasing supply of labour was available at a very cheap price. The same was true of the slave labour producing cotton, the chief raw material, in the southern USA and the West Indies.

II

The Nineteenth Century Apocalypse

In fact business was somewhat slow to develop after the long war which had disrupted normal trade and was followed by a depression as well as the beginnings of the severe trade cycles which were to become a disturbing feature in modern economic life. From around 1830 however the cotton industry in particular went ahead very fast. The consumption of cotton yarn rose at a staggering rate –

from	150,000	lbs	in	1820
to	250,000	,,	,,	1830
and	450,000	,,	,,	1840
	650,000	,,	,,	1850
	800,000	,,	,,	1860
	1,100,000	,,	,,	1870

All this entailed the rapid building not only of cotton mills but also of the houses, poor as they were, for the workers. A town like Oldham grew from 22,000 in 1801 to 72,000 in 1851 whilst Manchester more than quadrupled from 70,000 to 300,000. Even Leeds grew from 53,000 to 170,000 in the same period.

The new inventions and the growth in business activity led to, and were reinforced by, major developments in transport – in railways and steamships – so that the opportunities for trade to many parts of the world were greatly multiplied. North America and India were already opened up to British merchants and other continents, including Russia, South America and Australia were soon to follow.

Without these vast new openings for trade, British manufacture of textiles, particularly cotton goods, could not of course have developed as it did. An ample supply of cheap labour, including many Irish immigrants, meant that the workers in the new factories were paid wages which just about enabled them to keep body and soul together, but there was a strict limit to which money was available in England to buy the products of the factories. So the only way of maintaining the momentum of expansion made possible by the new technology, using ample supplies of raw cotton, power and labour, was to export. The following table shows what happened –

EXPORTS OF COTTON PIECE GOODS

(million yards)		(million yards)	
1820	300	1870	2700
1830	600	1880	4000
1840	1100	1890	5000
1850	1600	1900	5200
1860	2000		

FIG 2.   EXPORTS OF COTTON TEXTILES
QUANTITIES AND PRICES
1820–1880

A.   EXPORTS OF COTTON PIECE GOODS (MILLION YARDS)
(LEFT HAND SCALE) _____
B.   INDEX OF EXPORT PRICES FOR COTTON TEXTILES
(RIGHT HAND SCALE, 1820=100)   _ _ _ _ _

NOTE: THIS A SIMPLIFIED PICTURE SHOWING
APPROXIMATE POSITIONS REACHED AT
DISCRETE POINTS IN TIME. IT CONCEALS
LARGE TEMPORARY FLUCTUATIONS CAUSED
BY VARIATIONS IN TRADE.

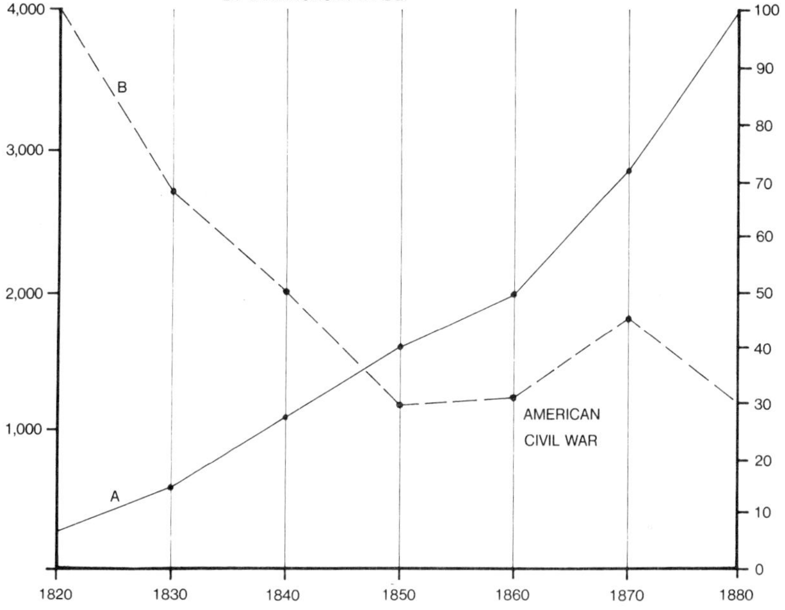

It is very evident that these great quantities of merchandise could only be sold by exporting a greater and greater proportion at lower and lower prices made possible by technical progress and cheap labour. Of course, the producers and merchants were competing with each other in the overseas markets which were hardly expanding as fast the goods were produced. It was not that there was much foreign competion but simply that the only way sales could be greatly increased was by reducing prices in conditions of severe competition between British merchants.

Between 1820 and 1850 the average price of exported cotton manufactures fell by some 70%. Thereafter there was little general change until a boom and the American Civil War raised prices by about 50% in the 1860s after which there was a further fall to about the 1850s level by 1880. The terms of trade (export prices ÷ import prices) fell from 170 in 1820 to 100 in 1860).

In no other country in fact was there a similar industrial development in the mid-nineteenth century and existing textile producers, as in India, were progressively put out of business by the flood of material from England. Thus at this time the English industrialists together enjoyed a near-monopoly position in the world, but they did not exploit it by controlling production and maintaining prices and there was no kind of mechanism or organisation for doing this. Exploitation of the markets was by quantity not high prices. But there were profits enough made by merchants and industrialists to fund the continuing expansion and indeed to invest overseas.

Already in the early part of the century and before, there had been a steady flow of foreign investment, the returns on which helped in investment at home, as well as funding an excess of imports over exports for most of the period. Much money was also made in transport with British shipping in a dominant position.

By about the middle of the century however a quite different situation had developed. The rising torrent of exports, even at their greatly reduced prices, could not be absorbed by overseas markets without a vast increase in British investment abroad. In part this was simply a question of lending money to the foreigners which they could use to buy British exports, particularly equipment and stock for the new railways, as well as for textiles. In addition a fair part of the money went to foreign governments and other organisations for general development purposes which in turn had the effect of widening the scope for British exports. It is by no means clear as to what extent this effect was specifically foreseen by industrialists and bankers, but the situation was certainly ripe for what took place. Without a doubt the mounting tide of exports of capital was a necessary condition for the flood of exports of goods. The following table summarises the story –

(£m annual averages)	Net Foreign Investment	Approx. Value of Exports
1831 – 35	6	40
1836 – 40	3	50
1841 – 45	6	54
1846 – 50	5	60
1851 – 55	8	85
1856 – 60	26	124
1861 – 65	22	145
1866 – 70	41	188
1871 – 75	75	240

(Between 1831 and 1871, Exports grew from 10% of gross national product to 25%. In the same period Imports grew from 14% to 30%)

The magnitude of the sums involved gives some indication of the profits made in the UK particularly in textiles. There was still much wealth left, therefore, to provide a high standard of living for large numbers of the upper middle class, and as the century progressed the returns on the overseas investment enhanced this process. Anyone who doubts this wealth should make a tour of the southern fringes of the greater Manchester area to observe the large numbers of mansions built by the cotton barons around a hundred years ago, many of them now being refurbished and resurrected as luxury apartments or private nursing homes for the elderly. This was the beginning of the period of *Upstairs, Downstairs*.

No review of the mid-nineteenth century, however brief, can avoid recalling a parallel development to that of spiralling textile production, which in fact substantially helped to make it possible, i.e. the building of the railways. Between 1830 and 1860 the principal country-wide network was constructed,

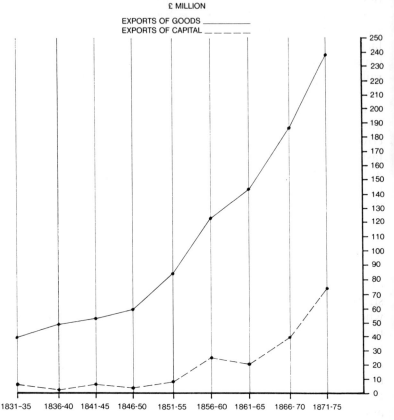

FIG 3. VALUES OF EXPORTS OF GOODS
AND OF CAPITAL 1830-1875
(FIVE YEAR AVERAGES)

£ MILLION

EXPORTS OF GOODS _____
EXPORTS OF CAPITAL _ _ _ _ _ _

some 9,000 miles at a cost of about £600 million or perhaps
£20 bn in 1989 money. It is in fact difficult to know the real
cost since so much was wasted in launching competitive
schemes many of which had to be abandoned. Extortionate
sums were paid to landlords and farmers for the necessary
land despite which local opposition often caused less
economic routes to be selected.

The London to Birmingham line, for instance, was due to
run close to Northampton, but the people in the area forced a
more westerly route to be taken to by-pass the town, thus
involving a tunnel of one and a quarter miles instead of one of

half a mile. Later another line was built via Northampton. But the M1 motorway found a route which did not require a tunnel at all.

It is really astonishing that so much capital was available at such an early stage to build the railways as well as the textile factories. It is perhaps no accident that the major export of capital from the late 1850s onwards came after the main railway investment. In any event we could not afford to build those railways today.

But what about the working classes? How did they fare amongst Victorian prosperity? It is extremely difficult to discover the true facts as to what really happened so long ago in a fast-changing industrial and social scene. There is a reasonable amount of information about wages but the data relating to living costs are much more difficult to evaluate in terms of their applicability to particular groups of people or indeed to that notional figure the 'average' man and his family.

As far as food supply, clearly the first priority, is concerned, there was no great revolution in British farming, but the repeal of the Corn Laws in 1846 opened the door for imports of wheat to make up the deficiency of home produce. The striking phenomenon is the general steadiness of the price of wheat until the last quarter of the century despite specific fluctuation in good or bad years. Consumption of other foodstuffs gradually increased. Meat was still a luxury, per capita consumption rising by no more than 10% per decade in the second half of the century reaching some 130 lbs p.a. by the end. The striking increases were in tea and sugar which after creeping up in the second quarter, rose strongly in the second half – tea by a factor of three to 6 lbs a head and sugar similarly to over 80 lbs. The increasing resort to sugar and tea was of course partly a reflection of easier supplies, so that by 1875 they together accounted for some 10% of the total import bill.

These simple facts are broadly consistent with the statistical evidence indicating a broad average increase of real wages of little more than 0.5% p.a. over the 50 years from 1820 to 1870. This gives us a general picture of a slow improvement of living standards, for long periods barely perceptible, at least compared with the depressed years after the Napoleonic Wars. But it is extremely difficult to say that most people were better or worse off than in the late eighteenth century, since life in the over-crowded industrial towns, with its extremely long hours of work for men, women and children, and its lack of decent sanitation, was a far cry from village life before the industrial age. It does seem however that whatever improvement developed during the mid-nineteenth century, it was nothing dramatic, and the principal betterment came in the last twenty years of the century as cheaper and more varied food poured in from the new continents.

It is hard to avoid the general conclusion that from the English national point of view the country's products and its labour were sold too cheaply during the mid-century decades. It would have paid most people much better if more invest-ment and effort had been applied to improving home agricul-ture and total food supplies, with the concomitant condition of lower textile production and higher prices. In modern con-ditions it would have constituted a classic case for raising the sterling exchange rate! This would have brought more food at lower prices without doing the damage to UK farming done by the flood of imports later in the century, Ironically this is the only period during the last two centuries when this could be true. At most other times sterling was too high, but in the mid-nineteenth century the spectacle was of vast numbers of English men, women and children herded almost like battery hens into mushrooming factories and houses to produce ever vaster and vaster quantities of cloth at ever lower and lower costs. It was a remarkable historical example of the fact that increased production very often does not benefit the producers.

III

Great Depression?

Looking back from the perspective of the late twentieth century it is hardly surprising that the frenetic pace of economic development in the middle fifty years of the nineteenth century could not be maintained. It was in fact the unique product of the coincidence of technological developments in textiles, power and railways which gave British capitalists a temporary near-monopoly in world trade and the opening-up of the continents.

As the century wore on and the railway boom slowed down, other countries in Europe, particularly Germany and North America, were learning to compete in the textile and other businesses and were developing their newer industries behind tariff and other barriers. Export trade became more difficult with lower margins: instead of growing at nearly 5% p.a. in the long boom years, the increase in the volume of exports fell to less than 2% p.a. The opportunities for vastly profitable overseas investment began to dwindle. So much capital had been accumulated and was available for new investment that lower returns had to be accepted with a higher proportion of the money going into projects at home rather than abroad.

Increased investment at home tended to bring more benefits for wage-earners, but the overriding benefit for most people came from the greatly improved supplies of food at much reduced prices resulting from the wider world boundaries and more developed trade, speeded by railways and steamships and later enhanced by the refrigeration of meat. The newly developed continents produced great quantities of cereals in particular so that by the 1880s prices were only about half their levels in the 1860s. Even meat prices fell by a quarter. Instead of food imports just supplying the additional population, they increasingly displaced some of the UK production, particularly of wheat, with imports supplying 75% of consumption by 1894 and home acreage falling by half. Imports of meat and livestock increased quite rapidly also, supplying about a third of consumption by 1895.

Imports of cereals came from far-flung countries, not only members of the Empire such as India, Australia and New Zealand but also from the Americas, Russia and the Danube and even from Northern Europe. Meat came increasingly from Australia and the Argentine as well as the established supply area of the Middle West of the USA. As Rider Haggard reported in 1903, even the less basic foodstuffs such as butter from France and Denmark, bacon and tinned meat from the USA, cheese from Canada, and Dutch eggs and margarine were appearing not just in hotels but even in village shops.

Clearly the British farmers had a hard time coping with severely falling incomes. They responded to the market pressures by making adjustments to their patterns of production and by cutting costs. By the use of some improved instruments such as the self-binding reaper and the double furrow, three-wheeled plough, they reduced labour costs, particularly of casual workers. They cut wages and negotiated some reductions in rents. Generally they survived but there was no revolution in farming methods, and only towards the end of the century did the enterprising ones turn to scientific farming and to such innovations as the breeding of pedigree cattle stocks for export.

The drift of the working people from the land to the cities inevitably continued in these conditions, but for those who had jobs on the farms, as well as in the factories, the advantages from lower food prices and more varied supplies were substantial even where wages were somewhat reduced. Real wages appear to have increased about 50% in twenty-five years – at an annual rate approaching 2%, three or four times the rate of improvement earlier in the century. With significant amelioration of working and living conditions, the late nineteenth century witnessed the real beginnings of a tolerable existence for the large urban working class.

Now it could be argued that these substantial benefits, representing the first notable improvement to living standards since the onset of major industrialisation, were the result, albeit belated, of the export of British capital to the developing

countries. This is however a most unlikely proposition. Substantial as the capital was in relation to the economic size of
the UK it was little more than a drop in the bucket of the total
of capital involved. No, the absence of British capital could at
most only have slightly delayed the overseas development and
perhaps made it a little more expensive.

It is however true that the large capital exports of the
nineteenth century did bring one considerable advantage
over the long period until the Second World War. The foreign
income earned by the assets created, even though much of the
money was lost, helped to pay for imports of food and raw
materials which were only partly covered by British exports
which increasingly struggled to compete with the rest of the
world. This deficit became much wider in the last part of the
nineteenth century.

(£m Annual averages)

	Deficit on visible trade	Invisibles; shipping financial Services	Investment Income	Current Balance
1830 – 39	– 17	+ 17	+ 6	+ 5
1840 – 49	– 25	+ 24	+ 7	+ 5
1850 – 59	– 32	+ 40	+ 15	+ 23
1860 – 69	– 60	+ 70	+ 25	+ 35
1870 – 75	– 65	+ 95	+ 45	+ 75
1889 – 84	–105	+105	+ 60	+ 60
1890 – 94	–125	+ 90	+ 95	+ 60
1900 – 04	–170	+110	+110	+ 50
1910 – 13	–195	+160	+175	+ 140

It will be observed that up to 1880, the net income from
shipping and financial services was more than enough to
cover the deficit on visible trade, so that all the income from
foreign investments was available for re-investment, together
with an increasing amount of new money. After 1880 however
the visible deficit became so large that invisible earnings were
insufficient to cover it. It was therefore necessary for some of
the foreign exchange income from investments to be effectively used to help to pay for the fast-growing quantities of
food and raw materials imports needed to keep the industrial
machine of Britain steaming ahead, allowing for the increasing demands of the labour force for a more tolerable standard
of life.

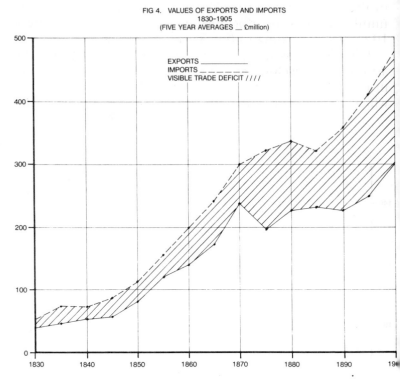

FIG 4. VALUES OF EXPORTS AND IMPORTS
1830–1905
(FIVE YEAR AVERAGES — £million)

EXPORTS _____
IMPORTS _ _ _ _ _
VISIBLE TRADE DEFICIT / / / /

Nonetheless, the income from overseas investments, just like the profits from enterprises at home, accrued to the well-to-do people who invested the money, not the mass of the people, and there is little doubt that, as the century progressed and moved into another, social inequality increased. By 1900 about 11% of the people received 50% of the national income. There were however significant improvements in living standards for many ordinary people particularly because of the growing numbers of better paid jobs as the economy became more complex and sophisticated. Increasing unionisation no doubt helped to raise real wages, and social legislation relating to hours and working conditions helped to reduce exploitation. Even living conditions were improved by legislation relating to sanitation and other standards.

There remained a substantial number of people at the bottom of the social groupings who were extremely poor partly no doubt because unemployment became a serious problem in the last decades of the century. Various surveys put the number in poverty or below the subsistence level at between 10 to 30% according to the standards adopted.

This then was the position reached in Britain after the astonishing development of the nineteenth century, in part inspired and certainly supported by the doctrine of free trade which had become virtually the subject of a moral crusade.

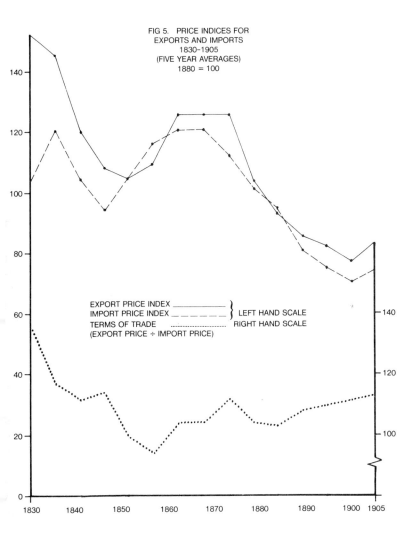

FIG 5. PRICE INDICES FOR EXPORTS AND IMPORTS 1830–1905 (FIVE YEAR AVERAGES) 1880 = 100

EXPORT PRICE INDEX _____ }
IMPORT PRICE INDEX _ _ _ _ _ _ } LEFT HAND SCALE
TERMS OF TRADE .... RIGHT HAND SCALE
(EXPORT PRICE ÷ IMPORT PRICE)

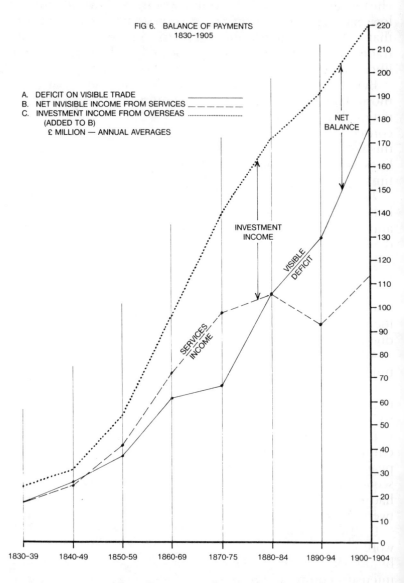

FIG 6.   BALANCE OF PAYMENTS
1830–1905

A.   DEFICIT ON VISIBLE TRADE
B.   NET INVISIBLE INCOME FROM SERVICES
C.   INVESTMENT INCOME FROM OVERSEAS
      (ADDED TO B)
      £ MILLION — ANNUAL AVERAGES

There is no doubt that free trade helped the business classes to make huge profits since it facilitated the provision of both the cheap raw materials for manufacturing industry, of which wool as well as cotton was increasingly important, as well as of cheaper food for the factory labourers thus keeping wages low. So dominant was the world primacy of English industry that it barely needed protection, anyway, though the odd trade which did, like silk manufacture, was sacrificed on the liberal altar.

By the latter part of the century, therefore, the country was thoroughly enmeshed in the tight and complex web of international trade from which it has never escaped, with major consequences through the twentieth century. The pattern of this web was as clearly defined as any of those criss-crossing lines woven by spiders as traps for their blundering victims.

The essence of the pattern was this. Large industries had been established particularly in textiles but also in heavy iron and steel, orientated towards railways, which in large measure depended on an increasing supply of raw materials from overseas. The labour for these escalating industries came from a fast-growing population which progressively depended on food supplies from all round the world. Fast as the export trade was growing it could not pay for all this vast amount of food and raw materials without the benefit of interest and dividends from overseas investments.

Add to this delicate situation some other hostages to fortune. Enormous social and economic inequality was evident in the huge profits in private hands much of which continued to be invested abroad. Aside from these, so much of the country's capital, managerial and just plain human resources were tied up in the original basic industries, that the country was ill-equipped to meet the challenging competition of other European countries, as well as the USA, which had come in on the second and protected wind of industrialisation and therefore had more than a head's start in the newer businesses of the twentieth century.

If British industrialists had been far-sighted enough they would have sought to maintain their leadership in world trade by transferring resources to the production of more capital intensive commodities or those incorporating a high degree of productive skill or expertise. In practice they allowed other countries to take the lead.

This was surely a scenario for economic crisis in Britain as the years went by. The world-wide competitive regime which soon developed required the most responsive and flexible reactions of the British economy, some 30 to 40% of which was directly related to international trade, a fearsome proportion. Even this proportion probably understates the real exposure of the British economy since it is related to the proportion of exports *or* imports to the gross national product but these are not entirely over-lapping and it is hardly an overstatement to insist that most of the economy has been quite closely affected by the vicissitudes of developments outside our control.

Relatively limited responses to these potent influences might conceivably have been reasonably adequate in a world as politically and economically stable as the nineteenth century. But the twentieth century was violently different, not just with two World Wars but also with world depressions and a vast enlargement of the world in trade terms, with enormous swings in currency exchange rates and indeed with major problems of inflation inflicted by oil cartels.

To cope satisfactorily with all these phenomena, given the exposed position of the British economy, would have required not just the most flexible and enterprising capitalists but also the most wise and discerning governments. Sadly there were many failures to attain these standards.

This was not by any means all. As the twentieth century progressed it became clear that the British class system which developed in the nineteenth century was singularly ill-equipped to assume the economic burdens of the twentieth. The lack of industrial professionalism among the moneyed classes has become a legend, no less true for that. These classes did however make one great discovery – the public school, with its basically classical education. This obsession set the tone for the elitist system of education that continues even today.

This was a tragedy not just for the moneyed classes but even more for the working classes for whom education was in any event doled out grudgingly throughout the period, a process which produced the secondary modern school after 1945 when education was supposedly democratised. It is not just that technical and vocational education has been sadly neglected but, more devastating still, the total quantity and quality of education for most of the people has been so low and so poor that we are severely handicapped in the sophisticated and technological era of the late twentieth century. All this explains many social and industrial attitudes. Even the managerial class in modern Britain is sadly uneducated in comparison with that of most of our competitors. (A more detailed account of the progress, or lack of it, in Education and Training is given in Appendix I).

In so far as the intelligentsia were attracted to the world of business, they generally preferred the remunerative commercial and financial operations centered on the city of London. Britain's pre-eminence in international trade and shipping and in lending money, led to a fast-growing business in financial services which stood on its own feet as a substantial contributor to the national wealth and particularly to foreign currency earnings. So it was understandable and justifiable that bright young men should be attracted to it. There were however some serious consequentials. First, the drain on the limited supply of educated people was such that even fewer were available for the more down-to-earth business of making things rather than money. Secondly, the banking and financial businesses developed so profitably and so independently and internationally that they became increasingly detached from industry. Thus the provision of finance for manufacturing investment in the UK was never a major interest of the banking community in the same way as it was in other countries and particularly in Germany.

IV

Into the Twentieth Century

If the nineteenth century had set the pattern for the twentieth, the latter was quick to show its colours. The dominant position of British industrialists, strongly challenged in recent decades particularly by the Germans and Americans from behind their strong tariff walls, was exposed to ever fiercer competition as the twentieth century dawned and progressed. In no trade was this more evident than in iron and steel which in Britain had been enormously stimulated by the demand of the railways. Much of this driving force ended in the 1870s when the railways network in the UK was completed; overseas demand, slackening as it did, especially after the 1880s, was increasingly met from the newer producing countries.

The German and American industrialists were far better organised to meet changing world requirements than the British. To whatever extent this was attributable to their tariff protection, it is undoubtedly true that in all major aspects such as forward planning, research and development, adoption of new techniques, scale of production, our industry was increasingly left behind. The result was that the British iron and steel exports actually fell during the 1880s and did not rise strongly again until around 1900. After 1900 production was greatly stimulated by the shipbuilding boom but imports took a large share of the extra demand and increased rapidly throughout the period from 1875. UK output of pig iron fell from 46% of the world total in the late 1870s to 14% just before the First World War, while the steel production share fell from 35% to 11%.

In the newer engineering industries, largely based on iron and steel, right through to the new motor vehicles as well as in chemicals, British industry was generally left behind, stranded in its conservative commitment to old lines of business and old ways of doing things. It was however rather more than

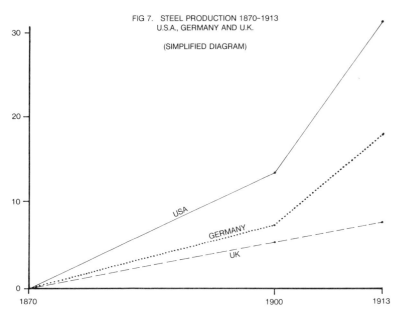

FIG 7.   STEEL PRODUCTION 1870–1913
U.S.A., GERMANY AND U.K.

(SIMPLIFIED DIAGRAM)

that. It has to be understood that the business initiative and enterprise which enabled Britian to dominate the world in the nineteenth century, although very considerable in its novelty and scale, was really quite straightforward by comparison with the more sophisticated trades which grew out of the original industrial breakthrough. Everything became more complicated and more variegated as well as very much more technological.

To be successful in the newer businesses required much greater product specialisation and development. More than that it involved more energetic marketing which it was less possible to entrust to merchants. With textiles, the principal requirements were adequate quality coupled with continously growing and more efficient production leading to lower prices. The business management techniques involved in highly competitive conditions in these processes were as child's play, especially in the British near-monopoly situation, to what was required in the newer and more developed industries. At no stage was there an adequate capability in depth in Britain, either in management or highly educated and trained manpower at the professional or craftsman level, to compete effectively over a wide industrial field in all these newer industries.

The plain fact was that the industries in which Britain had led the world and in which she still held an advantage, i.e. mainly textiles, coal, iron and steel, depended on the availability of substantial capital investment but more particularly of cheap low-grade labour which was obedient and compliant. The newer more sophisticated industries required more highly skilled and educated operatives capable of taking more independent action. In the older industries, substantial and successful business continued. In the newer industries, the British failure to provide both reasonable general education for the working people, and more specifically technical and vocational education, was entirely consistent with the failure of industrialists to perceive the longer term opportunities and needs including the requirement of educating their work-force. In this respect they were very different from the Americans and especially the Germans.

The period of fifteen years before the First World War has been described as 'climacteric' the great period of economic disilllusion for Britain when the marvellous engines of mid-Victorian growth, which had slowed to a more sustainable pace in the previous twenty-five years, actually ground to a halt. Certainly there were signs of a slackening of productivity growth in other countries, perhaps not surprisingly as the major benefits of the new nineteenth century technologies became somewhat exhausted before the even newer benefits of electricity and internal combustion had had time to bear much fruit. Raw materials, including coal, became scarcer and more expensive. But over and above such general factors, there were clear signs that Britain was falling behind other countries with its productivity growth stalling or even turning negative in the pre-war decade.

Already by 1910, labour productivity in Britain was on average only a little more than half that in the USA. Although trade union activity had begun by this time to be of some modest significance it can have had no real bearing on the comparison. There can therefore be no doubt that the reasons for this vast differential were deep-seated, by reference to the directions in which the country's industries were moving, the effectiveness of management and organisation and perhaps above all, the low value placed upon labour and the deficiencies in its quality arising from social conditions and from the inadequacies in the education and training it was deemed to merit.

Inevitably the greater increase in international competition drove industrialists to find ways of reducing costs or at least holding them down. This process became the more difficult because the early years of the twentieth century saw a significant reversal of the downward drift in prices, including food prices, which had lasted for twenty years. This is not the place to analyse all the reasons for this major change, but it is clear that the tidal wave of increased world food production in the later nineteenth century had somewhat subsided at a time when consumption requirements were growing in various countries. The long 'Great Depression' had constituted a 'one-off' step change in uncovenanted benefit for the British wage-earner, although it was a very substantial one, which was not quickly repeated.

So, as the cost of living turned upwards, there was a widespread demand for higher wages, strengthened by increasing organisation of trade unions especially among the skilled and semi-skilled workers. There were outbreaks of strikes including a national railway strike in 1911 and a national mining strike in 1910 and some modest wage increases were secured by workers who were already among the better paid. For the great majority however there was little if any recompense for the increased living costs so that there was a loss in average real wages of around 10% between 1896 and 1914, so reluctant were employers to accept a further narrowing in their profit margins beyond that enforced by increasing international competition.

Yet industry and trade remained hugely profitable and despite the real rise in working class standards in the late nineteenth century, income inequality undoubtedly increased in the early twentieth. There were therefore increasing sums available for investment from the surplus wealth of the moneyed classes. Total investment had fallen a little as a proportion of national income during the Great Depression but by the first decade of the century it was back to 12% or more, well up to the earlier level. The damaging fact for British industry was that over half this investment went overseas, and the benefit of this for the people at home was becoming increasingly difficult to discern. Certainly the vast majority of the money being lent overseas in the early twen_ieth century did not create a demand for British goods in the way which the great exports of capital did in the mid-Victorian boom period.

Overseas British investment which by 1900 had reached a net total of some £2 billion appears to have doubled by 1914 and in the last few years of the period was running at a rate close to £200 million a year. This vast sum, vast indeed for those days, represented approximately the annual profits on the total overseas investment. So easy was it for money to make money. This was not however a position which could endure since imports of physical goods still greatly exceeded exports, and the net earnings from shipping and financial services were not sufficient to cover the deficit. Thus not all the income from foreign investment could be re-invested abroad, and in later years more and more of it was required to pay for imports of food, raw materials and other goods. What might have been a steady process of adjustment was however soon disrupted by more catastrophic developments.

In the meantime the countries in the British Empire to which much of the capital went tended to retain the propensity to import British goods, and retained special lower tariffs than operated in most other countries. Thus the system of imperial preference was developed which had substantial advantages for the UK, particularly in relation to food supplies, until entry into the EEC destroyed the system It was in fact an essential part of the system that the UK should buy food from the overseas countries to give them the earnings to buy British manufactured exports.

The discrepancies between the rich and the majority of the population therefore grew steadily, despite the gradual improvements gained by a modest proportion of the working people. Some 12% of the working population were by now in domestic service. Low though their wages were, the working classes were in fact blamed by the moneyed classes for the flight of capital overseas where labour was cheaper and profits higher still! This was a stick which the rich found very convenient to use on the poor right through the twentieth century. In the 1980s it is echoed in the injunction to the unemployed to 'price themselves into jobs' which means competing with cheap labour in third world countries as well as, in Britain, providing additional labour to the expanding service trades i.e. working on low wages to serve the whims of the well-to-do.

For it is unemployment which has become an all-pervading sign of the times in the twentieth century. Of course it was by no means unknown in the nineteenth as the labour supply mushroomed from the rise in population and the flight from the land. But in the nineteenth century it could hardly be measured and was merely hidden in the swamp of misery of the bottom half of the population. But the new trade unions could count and soon governments were obliged to.

Unemployment fluctuated greatly with the trade cycle and clearly went above 10% at times. Although this was not the scourge it became in the 1920s and 1930s it was serious enough for the mass of workers on low wages who were always at risk from the vicissitudes of trade, which they scarcely understood and certainly could not control. Of course the capitalists were at risk as well, but they had 'limited liability' to protect them. Undoubtedly they did not get any fewer or poorer.

But it was becoming increasingly difficult for the establishment to keep the masses of labour under complete control. The very obvious fact of gross social inequality stimulated not just the growth of trade unions but also the extension of their activities into politics, especially because Parliament was passing laws to restrict the rights of the unions. The Labour Representation Committee, the forerunner of the Labour Party, began to get seats in the House of Commons; and the Liberal Government of 1906, despite its basic philosophical animosity to all government interference in the economic system, was driven to introduce the first old age pensions and national insurance provision. Even so, they made the working people pay most of the cost of these benefits. In this they were following the example of the Germans who were not just catching up but indeed moving ahead in so many ways.

However, these modest steps in social welfare did little to assuage the growing revolt by working people against the unfairness of their lot and the trade unions' power grew substantially so that the years just before the First World War constituted a period of more or less continuous industrial strife. In 1914 a great Triple Alliance was formed by the three big non-craft unions of the railwaymen, the miners and the transport workers. It would hardly be too much to say that revolution was in the air and the labour movement was certainly gearing up to claim a larger share of the profits of the booming industrial age.

Booming it certainly was, despite all the foreign competition. Exports, with a rise in volume of over 50% in fifteen years or so, were even out-pacing imports in the early twentieth century. There was a very significant feature of export sales, however, i.e. that the Germans were now buying British coal rather than manufactured goods on which they were levying a 25% tariff.

It is fascinating to ponder where this great contrast between enormous wealth and working class near-poverty would have led the British nation, already showing distinct signs of breaking apart, if war had not intervened. But it is difficult to avoid the conclusion that war itself was the logical outcome of the challenge by Germany to the industrial and financial dominance of the British Empire. One thing was for sure, nothing would ever be nearly the same after the most stupid and murderous war in history, which made no sense to or for the ordinary people.

And so the twentieth century in its earliest years was at once revealing the stresses and strains inherent in the economic pattern woven by the nineteenth century, and at the same time displaying its own distinctive characteristics of uncertainty and conflict. The vastly enlarged economic world created by technological innovation and expanding capitalism was so different from the one which emerged from the Napoleonic Wars as to be unrecognisable. Within a century waterpower had given way to steam and steam partly to internal combustion. Canals had given way to railways, which had opened up the continents as steamships had narrowed the oceans. Finally peace gave way to war. But the populous British in their small islands were stuck in the new century with the economic legacy of Empire and of a parallel dominance in industry and trade soon to be not merely impaired but fractured.

None of this could in any case last for ever but we have been behaving ever since as if we believed it had and should. For a while we could live off the stockpile of wealth and the advantages of Empire and indeed of language, even though the world owed us no favours, specifically not that of being its profitable monopolistic workshop. Until a second world war came, in fact, the moneyed classes did continue to draw a large tribute from imperial investment and the country as a whole was able to pay for both food supplies and raw materials. But it was an ominous fact that by 1914 Britain relied on imports for more than half its food.

Already the major industrial weaknesses which were to bedevil the country through the twentieth century had become very evident. The lack of application of technology in the newer industries and the associated short-sighted failure to invest in research and development were central to future developments. These would be compounded by the deficiences we have already noted in managerial abilities and education and particularly in the quantity and quality of education of the working people.

V

The Great War

The awful thing about the Great War of 1914–1918 is that
though a million Britons died on Flanders fields and many
more mourned for them, the country as a whole hardly suffered. One reason for this was that, compared with the second
round twenty-one years later, it was a very localised charnel
house in north-east France and Belgium where the PBI
slaughtered each other. Trade was certainly disrupted in western Europe but life in the rest of the world went on almost as
normal, except of course for the eastern front in Russia which
did not much affect Britain.

Even in Britain itself, the economic system was hardly disturbed for two years. The Government, believing essentially
in the free market system even in war, ordered its munitions
requirements from industry, persuaded the trade unions to
modify their working rules so as to permit dilution even by
growing hordes of women as the hordes of men disappeared
into the casualty lists and otherwise let things carry on more or
less as usual. After all the war would be over by Christmas –
but which Christmas?

After two Christmases had gone by, the going began to get
rather rough, however. Don't forget that Britain was the country, the only major country, which had allowed its agriculture
to decline to a level that supplied less than half the people's
food requirements. So when the German U-boats really
organised themselves to destroy Allied shipping, moderate
food shortages and high prices were translated into real
threats to survival, at least on reasonable nutritional standards. So, eventually, the government had to intervene to persuade the farmers to increase food production and particularly to switch from meat to wheat and other cereals which
could adequately feed many more people per acre. Even food
rationing was progressively introduced but starvation was

never close with an average of well over 3,000 calories a day per person being maintained. The average in these circumstances was more meaningful than is often the case since both troops and workers had to be adequately fed and fairer shares were necessary.

But with all the extra food produced at home, substantial imports were still necessary and of raw materials too. So how were they paid for? Well, of course they cost substantial shipping, much of it sunk, and many seamen's lives. In fact, despite all the hazards, total imports were virtually maintained in volume at the pre-war level. More astonishing still, exports had only fallen by 1917 to about half the 1914 volume.

The financial gap opened by the fall in exports was effectively made good by income from foreign investments which the government had begun to requisition in 1917 when the American loans made the measure largely redundant. A complex pattern of international loans, both to and from the UK, developed during the war years. We need not be concerned here with the details of these, nor the post-war settlement and it is sufficient to note that Britain retained most of her pre-war foreign wealth. What had not been possible, of course, was to add significantly to this wealth by further net capital exports.

So how did it all add up? The extraordinary development of the British economy in the century of peace had led to great overseas wealth built on the dominance of her manufacturing industry which required vast quantities of materials from overseas. It had also led to a depressed and shrunken home farming industry. The interest and dividends on the overseas wealth effectively paid, during the war, for the materials and food the country did not produce itself or buy with exports. Fortunate circumstance? Yes, but at some significant cost – notably the lives of many seamen.

The moneyed classes it is true had to draw in their horns a little for the duration. Their young men died too and their parents had more difficulty in finding enough servants. But huge profits were still being made since for most of the war munitions were supplied partly on normal contracts but increasingly on a cost-plus basis and profiteering was rampant. Farmers and landlords did well also. In any case, the newly-added wealth of the moneyed classes was being piled up for the future since the government relied mainly on borrowing to finance the war.

What then of the ordinary people? How did they fare? It may well be considered somewhat nauseatingly academic to calculate the arithmetical reduction in real wages caused by more than a doubling of food prices by 1917 and a very much smaller increase in average wages. This after all was not much of a problem to set against catastrophic death and mutilation on the battlefield. It must be remembered however that the ordinary people had little to spare and by 1918 they had endured a long twenty years during which, so far from making progress, their living standards had seriously fallen – not marginally but by some 10 to 20%.At least unemployment had disappeared for the duration and the people were reasonably fed.

Thus were the people conditioned for the post-war future when a new Jerusalem was to be built fit for heroes to live in. The war-time government drew up reconstruction plans which were little more than window dressing to bolster morale. But it did not prevent the rich getting richer and the poor getting poorer. After all, the market system was still king, if not god.

But private industry, operating in the market, partly controlled as it became during the war years, gained some distinct advantages which were to be of benefit to the country later. Perhaps the most vital was the realisation of production potential in meeting the demands of the war machine despite all the problems of wartime conditions and particularly of manpower. This quantitative stimulus was accompanied by qualitative improvements in terms of new engineering processes and techniques required for war production. Mass production methods were necessary for the manufacture of items such as shells and in general there were new incentives for imaginative management in doing new things on a large scale and overcoming problems of material shortage and labour dilution.

A major impact on industry came from the government, an entirely new development in a private enterprise culture. The Department of Scientific and Industrial Research was established to sponsor research not only in universities but also by industry. Some completely new industries, mainly with a high scientific content had to be established particularly to replace imports from Germany. The government even interfered in industry to encourage or impose improved processes and rationalisation as well as to introduce up-to-date accounting practices. Perhaps most significant of all was the stimulation of organisation and combination among manufacturers, including the formation of trade associations and arrangements for joint action. There were a considerable number of specific amalgamations, as in shipping, banking and railways, which were continued after the war.

This war-time demonstration of the scope for government action, although widely acknowledged as a special requirement in special conditions, was in a sense symptomatic of the major change in the economic and political atmosphere from the nineteenth century to the twentieth. The old certainties were sharply disappearing and the war accelerated the process. The trade unions and the Labour Party presented stronger challenges to the existing social order. Yet it was the weaknesses of the order itself which were becoming most apparent and were to dominate the 1920s and 1930s.

One of the nineteenth century certainties destroyed by the war was the stability of exchange rates of the major national currencies which had been tied to gold for most of the century. It is almost true to say that no one engaged in international trade had given a thought to any risk that the currency values in which they dealt could be subject to variation. Certainly there was no question of devaluing or revaluing sterling. Trade was not a matter for governments except in respect of the removal of barriers. True, Joseph Chamberlain had espoused the cause of tariff protection at the end of the century but made no progress except to display a sign that the old free trade certainties were beginning to be questioned as British trade dominance was threatened by other countries protecting their own industries.

However, the substantial damage to the established fabric of international trade inflicted by the war in Europe and the activities of the U-boats caused even the gold standard to fall. Even though, as has been explained above, the UK survived the trade difficulties of the war without great losses of reserves and overseas investments (although new investment was minimal), a major trade deficit developed because exports fell and the need for imports did not. Despite the cushion of income from existing foreign investments, the demand for sterling fell quite sharply in relation to that for other currencies and eventually the gold standard was effectively abandoned with sterling falling by some 20% by the end of the war.

In other respects, too, the disruptive effect of the war on trade was such as to disturb settled currency relationships, a fact which led to turmoil in exchange rates in the post-war years.

Nevertheless the overriding result of the war for Britain from the economic point of view was that her industry not only remained generally intact compared with the damage inflicted on our near continental rivals, but in many ways was strengthened and extended, even revitalised. Her empire was intact while Germany's was lost. It is true that the USA had grown much more in economic strength, but the world was big enough to contain that development and still offer a major new opportunity for the UK, in peace again, to recover lost ground in world trade.

It is the case, of course, that some of the expansion of British industry during the war was clearly superfluous in peacetime, particularly the production of munitions, but none of these expansions really caused major problems of post-war adjustment except, as in shipbuilding, where the false immediate post-war boom exacerbated the situation. Other industries such as textiles had continued to decline during the war but this was really consistent with the long term trend.

With the new recognition arising from the war situation of the vital importance of the major industries of the country as national assets which to some extent had to be managed by government, one might have supposed that wise government after the war would capitalise on the new opportunities offered for revival of Britains's trade position, with a stronger industrial base, and for improvement of the life of the people after deterioration over twenty years. How wisely these opportunities were to be used, we shall see.

VI

Between the Wars

In the introduction to his celebrated book '*The Economic Conse-quences of the Peace*' (1919) J.M. Keynes wrote –
'The power to become habituated to his surroundings is a marked characteristic of mankind. Very few of us realise with conviction the intensely unusual, unstable, complicated, unreliable, temporary nature of the economic organisation by which western Europe has lived for the last half-century. We assume some of the most peculiar and temporary of our late advantages as natural, permanent, and to be depended on, and we lay our plans accordingly. On this sandy and false foundation we scheme for social improvement and dress our political platforms . . .'
This striking passage was an introduction to Keynes' condemnation of the plan to extort enormous sums of money from defeated Germany by way of reparations for the damage caused by the war. However, its relevance to the whole economics of the inter-war years is astonishing. Indeed Keynes' historical prescience is wonderfully demonstrated by the applicability of his words right through to the 1980s.
One of the most important points made by Keynes was that reparations had to be paid across the currency exchanges so that they could only be fulfilled by the generation by Germany of a vast excess of exports over imports. In the short run this would clearly be impossible for a devastated economy and in the medium term would require the restoration of Germany to be a very healthy industrial country with a surplus of exports of German goods, a prospect many would not find it easy to welcome. Eventually Keynes' judgment was proved correct and very little of the reparations liability was in fact met, but the humiliation of Germany and the general violent depression of world trade led directly to Hitler and another war.

47

These developments demonstrated the more general truth of the Keynes' quotation above. The economic world which emerged from the Great War of 1914—1918 was in fact so different from that which had preceded it that many bright hopes of return to palmy days were dashed. But this was no historical accident since, as Keynes had so clearly perceived, the pre-war economic system was so inherently unstable that it would have required the greatest historical good fortune for it to have developed in a gentle and progressive manner for very long. Certainly it could not withstand the major shocks administered by the war, its disruption to established patterns of trade and the growth of new patterns of international indebtedness, all against the background of the vast enlargement of the economic world itself.

Nevertheless, this historical truth was not perceived by the British government and financial authorities, or if it was at all perceived, it was too uncomfortable a knowledge to be acted upon. For when politicians are in difficulty in a sea of doubt and uncertainty, they tend to return to the terra firma they know – and the same goes for industrialists.

The immediate post-war world boom, made inevitable by the rebound from wartime shortages and restrictions, was quickly followed by a slump with the economies of many countries in chaos and currency exchange rates in turmoil. The gold standard had been effectively abandoned virtually everywhere and its pre-war certainties which had formed the secure basis for international trade had shattered. So it is perhaps not surprising that British policy, from the end of the war onwards, had strongly favoured the restoration of the old gold standard. What is rather more difficult to understand in retrospect is why the authorities insisted on trying to restore it on a basis which would effectively increase the value of sterling back to its pre-war parity of almost five US dollars, an increase of some 25% from the level to which it had fallen during a brief period of 'floating' in 1919. The reasons for this policy cannot be fully explained here but they had much to do with national prestige and the creation of an atmosphere of confidence, coupled with the feeling that justice should be done to the 'rentiers' from pre-war whose returns were fixed in terms of sterling.

To justify such an increase in value, it was necessary to pursue a policy of deflation so as to reduce sterling prices. Inevitably this process caused many problems especially as falling prices are not conducive to business enterprise. The final stage was reached in 1924–1925 when a 10% increase in sterling was still necessary to reach the pre-war target. Keynes was bitterly opposed to the whole operation and wrote another of his pungently worded diatribes entitled 'The

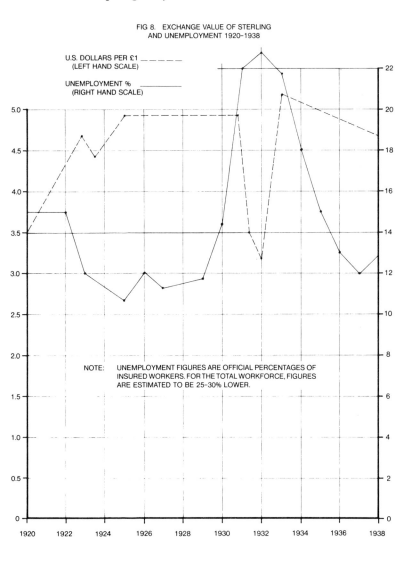

FIG 8. EXCHANGE VALUE OF STERLING AND UNEMPLOYMENT 1920–1938

NOTE: UNEMPLOYMENT FIGURES ARE OFFICIAL PERCENTAGES OF INSURED WORKERS. FOR THE TOTAL WORKFORCE, FIGURES ARE ESTIMATED TO BE 25–30% LOWER.

Economic Consequences of Mr Churchill' – who was the responsible Chancellor of the Exchequer.

Today we are all familiar with the consequences of an overvalued currency so that Keynes' patient explanation of the implications of a 10% reduction in sterling prices of our exports sounds all too obvious, but presumably it was not obvious to Mr Churchill. Of course if prices are to be forced down within the country, Keynes explained, it is necessary to drive down wages first and expect the workers to take the promised fall in prices on trust. (He also explained that deflating the economy is achieved basically by creating unemployment, a fact which politicians of today appear to want to conceal). Undoubtedly this policy was a recipe for disaster, leading to a major coal strike and then to the General Strike of 1926. The more enduring consequence was that Britain lost out by not participating at all fully in the world economic recovery which lasted until 1929.

Already in the 1920s the traumas of trying to cope with the chaotic economic world of trade deficits and fluctuating exchange rates, together with violent changes in the levels of economic activity, had significantly reinforced the late nineteenth century tendency towards protectionism, particularly as the newer industrialised countries sought to build up their manufacturing bases behind tariff walls. Even in Britain some tariffs had been introduced during the war, mainly to curb the level of imports particularly of agricultural products, but also of some luxury goods. Under this latter heading the nascent motor car industry was protected by a 33⅓% import duty which continued through almost the whole interwar period and undoubtedly helped to establish a substantial industry in the UK including such well-known names as Austin-Morris and Ford.

The US stock market crash of 1929 and the deep world-wide slump which followed turned even the UK protectionist. It is an interesting point that even Keynes, an ardent free trader until 1931, had changed his mind in favour of a general import tariff until finally the decision was taken in the autumn of that year to abandon the gold standard, devaluing sterling by 25%, which had a much greater protectionist effect. Even so, it became clear before long that this was not enough to revive British industry and many protectionist and interventionist measures were taken. Bank rate was reduced to 2% in 1932 and a slow but steady recovery followed into the boom of 1937.

The whole world in fact, after various fruitless efforts to find a new international monetary regime to facilitate trade, was moving into autarky. The strong winds of international competition in the chaotic financial and currency climate of the 1930s were regarded as far too strong for the major countries to expose their domestic economies to them. So Britain, among others, moved towards self-sufficiency. The volume of exports fell progressively throughout both the 1920s and 1930s until it was about 30% lower. Imports on the other hand actually increased by some 20%. However, despite all the problems, the national income increased substantially during the period partly because of major technical progress, so that whereas before 1914 both exports and imports accounted for well over 30% of national income, by 1938, the percentage for both was down by about half.

It may seem very odd that the quantity of imports should increase so much in comparison to exports, and it must be remembered that the measures of these volumes cannot be exactly accurate. However, the essential point is that the terms of trade, the relationship of general export prices to import prices moved strongly in favour of Britain over the whole period. This development, not unconnected with the poor economic condition of the developing countries whose food and material products were falling in price, was one of the results of the great slump and also a cause of its intensification.

Two other major aspects of this great improvement in the terms of trade – by an astonishing 40% compared with the immediate pre-war period, must be noted. First, the standard of living of most people in the UK received a great boost despite unprecedented levels of unemployment. Secondly, the UK was saved from what would otherwise have been a major balance of payments problem. This would have been the case in spite of the fact that the continuing benefit from returns on foreign investment, although only about half the pre-1914 level, provided a significant cushion allowing the value of imports of goods generally to exceed that of exports.

The British export trade had suffered badly until 1931

because of the over-valuation of sterling in an unsettled economic world, descending into deep depression at the end of the period. When new policies were applied by the UK government in the 1930s, the world had become essentially protectionist so our export business had little chance to revive significantly. How different all this was from the century up to 1914 when trade hardly ever went down, only upwards at a staggering rate.

There were of course some export successes in the newer industries in the 1930s but basically the country turned, for the first time in peace, to the task of providing for itself, by no means unsuccessfully. Total industrial production which by 1924 was perhaps 5–10% above the pre-war level and rose by a further 10–15% by 1929, then fell back to the 1924 level in 1931, but achieved another increase of about 50% by the boom year of 1937. It is interesting to recall something of what happened in particular industries.

The mainspring of the industrial revolution and of the dominance of Britain in the mid-nineteenth century had been the cotton industry. The opening-up of the world and its movement towards autarky ensured that many other countries would learn the comparatively simply technology of the textile business and make cloth for themselves. Further it was relatively easy to apply cheap labour to the job, as in India and Japan, and make textiles at low prices for other people. For India it was an ironic tit-for-tat. Her own textile industry had been virtually destroyed by cheap British imports in the nineteenth century. In the twentieth century cheap Indian production severely damaged the British industry. It speaks volumes for the generosity of the English working man that when Gandhi visited Lancashire in the early 1930s he was wonderfully well received.

For the cotton industry had suffered worst of all, with production down to less than half the pre-war level by 1930 and not rising thereafter, whilst exports fell by 75% in volume by 1938. Not suprisingly, employment fell by some 40%. Increasingly the government was driven to intervene to assist and protect the industry, to the point where, in the later 1930s, it arranged a statutory reduction of capacity and a compulsory cartel to raise prices.

All the major older industries, including iron and steel,

shipbuilding, coal and older engineering businesses, suffered to a substantial extent and were the subject of government regulation or assistance.

But it would be wrong to concentrate too much on the old declining industries since the now irresistible forces of technological invention and development were radically changing the world both economically and in consumption. Indeed, industrial enterprise now had to apply itself to the development of technology as never before, with government playing a stimulating and supporting role. Perhaps the most significant underlying technological change was the exploitation of electricity which transformed most industrial production and promoted new important trades such as electrical engineering.

The internal combustion engine which, like electricity, had begun its spectacular progress before the war also blossomed out in the 1920s and 1930s as mentioned above. Whilst it could hardly be said to command a mass market its importance was growing fast under the protection of the import tariff and even achieved significant exports although these never amounted to more than about 15% of production with other countries developing their own industries behind tariff walls.

Of the other newer industries the most important was the chemical business and the related chemistry-based industry of man-made fibres using cellulose. Both these industries prospered on the basis of monopoly and cartel organisation under the familiar names of ICI and Courtaulds respectively. In each case a high degree of control over the UK market was supported by strong links with the principal producers abroad and particularly in Europe. It would be hard to deny that these increasingly non-competitive operations achieved substantial technical and commercial progress which would have been most unlikely in exposed free market conditions, certainly in the circumstances of the period. There were similar stories in soap (Lever) and glass (Pilkington).

In the nineteenth century and the early twentieth century, exports had been the most powerful engines of economic growth for Britain. It is perhaps significant that in the early 1930s it was the building industry, particularly house building, which was the principal centre of expansion, stimulated no doubt by interest rates down to 2%, radiating its effects over a wide field. This development was symptomatic of an economy turned in on itself and less subject to the vicissitudes of international trade. How changed things were from the nineteenth century apocalypse!

For the farmers of Britain, the 1920s were a continuation of the trend since 1875, broken only briefly by a rise in prices in the first decade of the twentieth century. Some protective measures were carried over from the war but the cost of price support became so prohibitive in the early 1920s, when world prices slumped in the post-war depression, that they were all abandoned. The farmers were able to help themselves to some extent by flexibility in switching away from cereals to the meat and dairy products for which there were increasing demands as standards of living rose, not least because of the fall in food prices.

Even so, the proportion of British food consumption produced in the UK continued to fall during the 1920s, even for meat, so that by 1930 half of the consumption of both meat and eggs was supplied from abroad, 60% of cereals and 80% of butter and cheese, as well as nearly all the sugar. In this period the government did take the initiative in establishing a sugar beet industry in the country which achieved some success in the 1930s.

As with manufacturing industry, it was in this later decade that protection, subsidy, guaranteed prices and market organisation played a significant part in stemming the downward drift. In fact the extent of government intervention was far more extensive than for most industry. There were however particular difficulties about reducing imports too drastically since many of them came from the Empire countries under the system of imperial preference. But at any rate the downward drift of British agriculture was halted and some modest increases in production achieved especially late in the 1930s.

Nevertheless, dependence on imports of food was still very heavy at this time with little change from the proportions quoted for 1930 except for sugar and eggs. The drift of labour from the land continued as efficiency grew.

Not that there was anywhere for the workers to go. The gross waste of industrial and agricultural resources throughout the inter-war period was of course exemplified by the plague of unemployment. The totals were horrific in themselves, rising to an early peak of 16% in 1921 in the post-war slump, falling a little to 11% before the return to the gold standard in 1925, which sent it quickly escalating to 22% in 1931. Thereafter there was a gentle recovery back to 12% in 1937. [These are the official figures for insured workers. For the total workforce the percentages are some 25–30% lower.]

Within these totals there were special stark tragedies of vast numbers of people trapped in the areas where the older industries were concentrated and with few skills or opportunities for moving to the newer industries especially as there were in any case far too many people looking for jobs everywhere. There were not many working people who escaped at least the risk of unemployment.

J M Keynes was almost alone in believing that major inroads could be made in unemployment by government action aside from protecting and assisting private industry. In the 1929 General Election he had, with Hubert Henderson, written a trenchant pamphlet in support of Lloyd George who had undertaken to reduce unemployment by a programme of public investment, arguing particularly strongly against the notion that this would 'crowd out' private investment. (The same nonsense notion has been put about in the 1980s). But this was before the great slump of 1929–31 swamped all reason. So the country stumbled through the 1930s with *ad hoc* measures to assist decaying and growing industries alike.

The statistics indicate that the level of real wages for those in work increased by some 30% between 1913 and 1938, but the effect of unemployment reduced the figure to around 20% per member of the total workforce. Most of the improvement came from technical progress and lower food prices. Since the latter phenomenon was more apparent in the 1920s, most of the statistical improvement in real wages came then when money wages had fallen but not as much as prices: only in the 1930s was there a slow rise in money wages.

Where then had Britain arrived, as the Second World War approached? Obviously, to a very different situation from that the country occupied in 1914. The once-proud workshop of the world with a vast export trade was reduced to being a modest member of the comity of nations all looking after their own interests on the narrowest of fronts, retreating into self-sufficiency as the safest of havens amid the foul winds of international trade. Even so, we were still one of the largest world exporters of manufactured goods, second only to – yes, Germany, which goes to show what a different world it was. It is also a mark of how far we had yet to fall before, in a much more expansive world fifty years later, Britain was not a net exporter of manufactures at all.

Even the limited objective of selling enough to buy essential imports to feed its people and supply its industry with enough materials was barely being accomplished at a level of trade so low that exports were a mere 15–16% of total production. With all its protection and subsidy British agriculture produced less than half the nation's food, for even the benefit of Empire had at this point become almost a burden in the form of a liability to accept its food products. Yet a substantial deficit on visible trade was financed by the still valuable earnings on imperial investments of long ago, together with the so-called invisible earnings of shipping and financial services.

In terms of technology and organisation the country's industries were still well behind those of at least Germany and the USA despite some encouraging developments. In terms of education and training, the country's people were poorly provided, in both quantity and quality, with the virtually whole of its education geared to elitist classical education of the few with substantial disregard of not only the technologies but also of the science and practice of management of industry. The moneyed classes, many of them living still on the easy money of the nineteenth century, were not very interested in the dirty business of making goods and money in the twentieth. For gentlemen the more suitable occupations were the law, the civil services, including the imperial service, and the church.

This then was the country which now had to wage the biggest war of all for a year or two more or less on its own and then, bearing the cost of that war, climb back into solvency, viability, self-respect – and full employment. These most formidable tasks would certainly require qualities of the ordinary people which they themselves knew they possessed but which they had rarely had the opportunity to demonstrate in the past. They would require also qualities of business enterprise in the managerial classes which very few had displayed in the inter-war years. For we believed, or professed to believe, in free trade as well as private enterprise, in a world which, having grown much wider in the last century, would quickly grow much smaller.

This brave new world would, above all, require British industry to develop new products for potential customers around the world, which involved not only going to find out what these foreigners wanted, to learn their customs and languages and, in order actually to sell to them, in fact to camp out on their doorsteps. Very few Britons had done this kind of thing in the past and many would consider it all somewhat *infra dig*. Perhaps it was not too surprising that the dog did not talk too well – the miracle was that it talked at all!

VII

The Second World War and Recovery

We are not here concerned with the economic intricacies of the war and its management but only to draw out the major points relevant to Britain's general economic development and particularly to the emerging pattern of foreign trade.

The first major point to be made is that the second war was even more demanding in terms of production and diversion of resources than the first. This time the production requirements were not only greater but also more sophisticated – for many thousands of aircraft for instance – and considerable impetus was again given to the engineering industries. Altogether, the country was more thoroughly and efficiently organised than before and indeed than any other combatant country, including Germany. Government control of and engagement in industry, although generally effected through allocations of material and labour, was introduced more quickly and went much further than in the first World War.

Agriculture too was managed through a mixture of controls and financial incentives so that the proportion of food produced at home went up from about a third to nearly a half with a great shift towards cereal production. The margins of survival were narrower than in 1914–18 with strict food rationing involving very low levels of consumption of meat and dairy products in particular. Complex calculations were required to achieve a flexible balance between production at home, the financial costs of buying from abroad and the availability of shipping space as more and more ships were sunk by the enemy.

The external financial aspects of the war were extremely involved. Inevitably about half of the country's export business had eventually to be sacrificed and, since the balance of payments was already in deficit before the beginning of the war, even with the benefit of dividends from foreign investments, it was quite impossible to finance necessary imports on a current basis. Most of the remaining foreign investments had to be sold and large debts to the empire and other countries in the so-called 'Sterling Area' were incurred. Dollar debts were accumulated with the USA although the 'Lend-Lease' programme provided essential relief.

Apart from the direct financial costs of the war which could be measured in terms of sales of assets and accumulated debts, there were almost incalculable losses in terms of destruction by bombing, the running down of capital assets in transport and public services because of neglect of repair and renewal and the vast disruption of continuity in production, both for home consumption and exports, involved in directing the maximum effort to war production. Even more difficult to assess, though no less damaging in its nature, was the dilution of labour resulting from the loss of experienced and skilled men to the forces with the huge consequential gap in some industries in training and developing the skilled labour force which would be required in the sophisticated industries of the mid-century.

All these costs and losses represented very substantial minuses to set against the plusses of enlargement of the engineering and allied industries as well as metal manufacture and the iron and steel and chemical industries, which was accompanied by an improvement of the quality of their operation. It was fortunate that in the main it was the newer industries which benefited.

The very considerable material and financial assistance provided by the Americans, quite apart from their eventual entry into the war after the Japanese attack on Pearl Harbour, put the UK under major obligations as to their financial behaviour in the post-war world. The USA had for some time developed a dominant position in the world economy. With enormous natural resources in relation to population, this was hardly suprising. Moreover, their large home market had no doubt helped to inspire the adoption of mass production techniques – associated frequently with the name of Henry Ford. So it was not unexpected, perhaps, that the USA in the mid-twentieth century saw opportunities for expansion into world trade to rival those enjoyed by the dominant British in the nineteenth century.

Certainly the USA, having developed its industries originally behind a tariff wall, had increasingly come to believe in the merits of free trade and non-discrimination. So they obliged Britain to give a number of vital undertakings about compliance with these doctrines. A specific commitment about non-discrimination was understood to relate particularly to abandonment of the system of imperial preference. Even during the war Britain was supposed not to incorporate in exports any materials supplied under lend-lease, lest American materials should be used to compete against American exporters! The plain fact was that the US was already wealthy enough to carry the cost of their involvement in the war by extra production without affecting standards at home and the American people found it difficult to appreciate how difficult, if not desperate, the British situation had become. But economic and financial dependence on the US became a fact of life so there was little the UK could do to resist the onerous conditions imposed.

Indeed it became very obvious that when the war was over the UK, and even Western Europe as a whole, would not be in a financial position to survive on their own without an economic disaster surpassing that of the war itself. The UK position may be summarised in terms of the balance of payments position and the accumulated debts. In 1938 and 1939 the country's visible imports had cost some £850 million p.a. of which visible exports had covered only some £470 million. Invisible earnings, including interest and dividends yielded some £250 million (net). By 1944 exports had fallen to 30% of the pre-war level so that even in 1945 they were worth no more than £400 million which included some recovery during the transition to peace. Imports fell too by over a third in volume by the end of the war and had been reduced in value to only £650 million in 1945, after costing much more in the interim, because of the increasing free deliveries under lend-lease.

Clearly the prospect for the post-war years was daunting in the extreme. If imports were to return to anything like their pre-war level the adverse balance on visible trade would be at least £600 million and might well be much more and the government was spending some £300 million p.a. abroad in 1945 and 1946. Foreign investments had been substantially reduced, so net invisible earnings could hardly be much more than £100 million.

In addition to selling overseas assets worth some £2 billion, Britain accumulated debts of almost £3½ billion. Even these vast sums were exceeded in total by gifts from the US and Canada.

This then was the sombre position in which total war had left Britain in 1945 when the sudden ending of the war against Japan triggered the termination of lend-lease by the USA. Even worse, the overseas trade position was exacerbated by the rise in prices of world agricultural production caused by wartime disruption and the urgent need of much of western Europe for food supplies to relieve the low levels of nutrition to which the war had reduced the people. So the terms of trade turned decisively against Britain. Thus, to return Britain to something like a viable life it was calculated at the end of the war that it would be necessary to increase the volume of exports by 75% above pre-war levels by 1950. In the meantime substantial deficits would continue to be incurred.

Whilst so much was similar to the 1918 situation, in terms of British impoverishment and financial problems, much else had changed. This was partly a question of learning from the mistakes of last time, including the upheavals of the inter-war period and partly from a wholly different political and economic philosophy. There was of course an international as well as a national dimension to all of these matters, and this effectively meant mainly the USA and the UK.

There was a fair measure of agreement between the wartime governments in the two countries that international trade needed to be greatly enlarged compared with the restrictive and autarkic pre-war period. The basic conditions for achieving this objective appeared to be the establishment of reasonable stability of currency exchange rates, without the rigidity of the old gold standard and an improvement in international liquidity which would enable the nations to avoid restrictive trade practices such as tariffs or specific restrictions on imports. As indicated above, the views of the US had by now become more strongly in favour of free trade than those of the British but J M Keynes, no longer regarded as a heretic and established as a power in the land, was able to negotiate some concessions leading to the famous Bretton Woods Agreements of 1944 which established the International Monetary Fund and the World Bank.

The principle of the IMF was that member countries would subscribe funds which could be used to provide loans to those members who ran into short-term foreign exchange problems. Exchange rates would only be altered to deal with fundamental structural problems and would require permission in advance. The principle of non-discrimination in international trade was always emphasised by the US and, like a commitment not to place restrictions on currency payments, was enshrined in the Agreements. Further undertakings to reduce tariffs and trade restrictions were incorporated in the General Agreement on Tariffs and Trade in 1947.

Quite apart from these agreements, Britain needed a large loan from the US to tide over the immediate post-war years and this was duly negotiated. Consistently with the major trade agreements, Britain had to accept an undertaking to permit free convertibility into dollars of the vast sterling debts (Sterling Balances) accumulated during the war. When this was reluctantly honoured in 1947 it caused immediate financial disaster and had to be hurriedly suspended. Eventually these bilateral arrangements between the US and Britain were superseded by the great Marshall Plan by which the US effectively gave the necessary financial aid to put Western Europe back on its economic feet.

If economic liberalism was the obligatory doctrine governing the international dimension for Britain after 1945, the internal philosophy was very different. For one thing, the lessons and experience of the first war and its aftermath had created a determination to do much better this time. The political atmosphere which was to lead to the overwhelming election of a Labour government in 1945, had already ensured during the war the making of detailed plans for full employment and effective social welfare, for public housing, better education and a national health service. Keynes and Beveridge reigned supreme and if there were some people in the Coalition war-time government and in the moneyed classes who were interested only in paying lip-service to these liberal and reformist (even socialist?) doctrines, the election of the new government was to ensure that serious and earnest efforts were made to give effect to the war-time promises.

No doubt many mistakes were made in the first five years of peace as the government grappled with all the problems of shortage of foreign exchange, of fuel and many other things, as well as controlling the ever-present risk of inflation. It was not so much a lack of administrative tools since many of the war-time controls such as allocation of scarce resources like coal and building materials and labour, as well as rationing of clothes and food, were continued over most of the period. It was much more a question of how best to use the available powers in pursuit of a fair number of sometimes conflicting objectives as well as to persuade capital and labour to co-operate. One vital objective was kept well in mind: despite the many calls on current resources, the need to encourage investment was well understood with interest rates down at 2½%.

In 1949 balance of payments difficulties and a run on sterling persuaded the government to devalue the currency from $4.03 to $2.80 to the pound, which seemed excessive at the time and afterwards, tending as it did to move the terms of trade even further against the UK. However the devaluation was certainly effective in restoring confidence and exports rose even faster so that the 75% increase target was duly met and a substantial balance of payment surplus achieved in 1950. Perhaps the biggest mistake made by the Labour government was to adopt a large rearmament programme because of the Korean War. Aneurin Bevan and Harold Wilson resigned nominally because of the imposition of health service charges to help to pay for the arms programme but in reality the issue went deeper since the 'rebels' believed with some justification that the new war effort was unnecessary and unaffordable.

Although 1951 consequently saw fresh economic problems, including a substantial trade deficit, these were mainly associated with a new rise in world prices particularly affecting British imports and the problems were not long-lived so that, ironically, after an initial crisis largely resulting from the Korean War, the new Conservative government which took over late in 1951 had a fairly easy passage. They inherited an industrial production level which by 1950 was already about a third greater than before the war, with a considerably greater increase in productivity than in the 1930s, despite (or because of?) the maintenance of full employment.

The working people obviously benefited from the availability of jobs and by working long overtime hours were able to enjoy significant improvements in living standards as well as better welfare standards. The basic poverty affecting a large proportion of people in the 1930s had effectively been alleviated. There was dissatisfaction that income standards were not higher, but this was really a measure of the difficulties inherent in the country's situation. The Trade Unions were remarkably modest in their wage claims apparently because of the new spirit of those years.

What then of the industries which provided all these jobs? It should be emphasised that although the government nationalised some major industries such as the public utilities like electricity and gas as well as coal and railways, manufacturing industry remained essentially in private hands although having to work within a diminishing framework of controls. Perhaps progress was somewhat too easy for private industry in this period of pent-up demand, but in general a good recovery had been made from the war and a reasonable launching pad for a more normal period of peace established.

The revitalisation and expansion of the 'newer' industries, such as engineering, metal manufacture and vehicles, as well as the chemical industry, which had taken place during the war were extended into the recovery period. Chemicals were outstanding with a doubling of production by 1950 while engineering and vehicles were about 50% up on pre-war level with lower employment. But iron and steel were still important, albeit with new demands, and kept pace with the general expansion of industry.

A most significant development was represented by the treatment of agriculture which was directed towards even greater production levels than attained during the war in order to save even more imports. The Agricultural Act of 1947 established the system of guaranteed markets and prices, subject to annual price reviews, for the main farm products. This assurance of stability for the industry was accompanied by various measures to improve efficiency, including tax concessions as well as advice provided by the National Advisory Service and County Agricultural Executive Committees. By these means the target of a 20% increase in production in five years was achieved, raising total output to about 50% above the pre-war level.

It can hardly be doubted that recovery from the Second World War was far better organised than the chaotic lurch back into the free market after 1918. If industry was not better managed than it was and not more prepared for meeting international competition when the enemy countries, as well as more friendly nations, recovered from the war, any failings must surely have stemmed from more deep-seated causes than the manner in which the post-war recovery was achieved.

The people, too, were in much better heart than for a long time despite all the shortages, of which housing remained most important. So great in fact was the total revolution in outlook that the economic and social structure which had been created out of war and its aftermath was only to be marginally modified during a long period ahead.

VIII

The Consensus Years: 1950s and 1960s

The period from 1951 to 1979 has become known as the age of consensus because the social and economic revolution effected by the war and the post-war Labour government was not seriously challenged and because all governments in the period followed broadly similar policies to deal with similar problems. From the social point of view a modest but significant shift towards greater equality of incomes was reinforced by high taxation on high incomes and by the greatly strengthened welfare system. The continuing emphasis on full employment and economic growth as aims of economic policy supported the social changes.

It is true that the Conservative governments who took office from 1951 onwards believed less in controls or any kind of involvement in private industry, whereas the Labour governments believed more in planning and eventually in incomes policies. Yet they all accepted that private enterprise would remain free to operate over the greater part of the economy with only some major utilities plus coal and transport in public ownership leaving iron and steel as the major disputed territory. Agriculture remained under a stabilised economic system of guaranteed prices and sales until in the 1970s the EEC system took over. Overseas trade remained basically open and uncontrolled, and the sterling exchange fixed until 1967.

The essential problems which dominated the period were, first, the balance of payments and secondly, and increasingly, inflation.Although the balance of payments was restored to temporary surplus soon after the Korean war, there was never a sufficient margin of safety to act as a cushion when anything went wrong. The need for a cushion was particularly acute because of the existence of the large sterling balances held in London by British Commonwealth and other countries who could decide to run them down at short notice particularly when economic problems arose, as they often did.

Inflation also was a problem which only slowly crept up on the country after 1951. It is difficult to be sure what caused it but one school of thought would certainly connect it with full employment and the slow realisation by organised labour of the strength of its bargaining power in these conditions. Couple this tendency with the mid-twentieth century-acquired expectation of a steadily rising standard of living based on technical progress and the fruits of large scale production, and one can clearly see the potential for trouble if things went wrong even temporarily. Well, what could go wrong? In fact it is difficult to know where to start since in economics everything seems to depend on everything else, but trouble arose from anything which disrupted the orderly progress of economic expansion in such a way that the expectation of a continuous rise of real wages was disappointed.

Most often this kind of trouble arose from Britain's position as a small group of islands in the midst of a vast expanding economic world. Not just expanding but changing fast as the devastated countries of Europe and the Far East quickly reorganised themselves. Of these, Germany and Japan became ever stronger as, with determined government planning and support of industry, they organised themselves to meet the requirements of the new economic world. The growing competition from such countries in international markets, coupled with the vulnerability of the British balance of trade, led to increasingly frequent and severe problems for sterling. Already in the mid-1950s the delicate balance was being disturbed and in 1957 the first serious threat of a run on sterling caused the government to put the brakes on the economy with an increase in interest rates and a tighter monetary policy. Bank Rate went up to the unprecedented post-war level of 7% after a norm of 2% up to late 1951.

Thereafter it seemed almost inevitable that every few years a government belief in economic recovery inspired an expansionist policy which soon brought in a flood of imports causing a balance of payments crisis and the risk of devaluation of sterling. Each time this happened the government reversed course and took measures to depress the economy and to restrict imports. For instance, following the crisis measures of

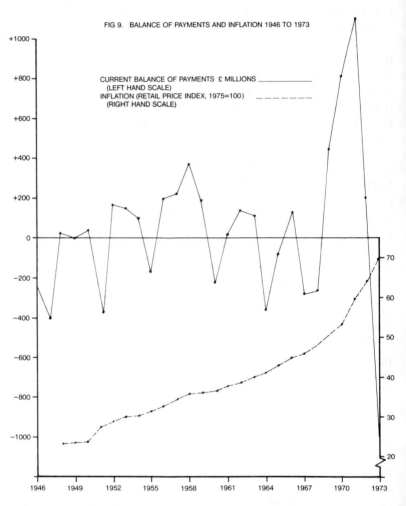

FIG 9.   BALANCE OF PAYMENTS AND INFLATION 1946 TO 1973

CURRENT BALANCE OF PAYMENTS £ MILLIONS _____
(LEFT HAND SCALE)
INFLATION (RETAIL PRICE INDEX, 1975=100) _ _ _ _ _ _ _
(RIGHT HAND SCALE)

1957, the economy was clearly depressed in 1959 with a favourable balance of payments and unemployment up to 2.8%, so an expansionary budget was introduced. For a year or so all went well with industrial production up 10%, but in 1960 it was necessary to apply the brakes, gently at first but more sharply by 1961 when a financial crisis developed requiring international loans of over £1 billion to be taken and bank rate to be raised to 7% again in order to save sterling. The additional national indebtedness was clearly a millstone round the neck of the future economy.

By 1964, election year, the whole cycle had been repeated and after thirteen years of Conservative 'stop-go' the incoming Labour government was obliged to take vigorous action to deal with a record balance of payments deficit of almost £500 million. Apart from tax increases, a 15% surcharge was imposed on all imports of manufactured and semi-manufactured goods, amidst much international opposition.

Thus the Labour government was effectively forced to abandon its brave plans for a national plan to bring about controlled expansion of the economy. The weakness of the balance of payments had by now become recognised as chronic, and economic policy was driven to be more or less continuously depressive and deflationary. Despite all the efforts to protect sterling, the overdue devaluation came in 1967 – down to $2.40 to £1 from $2.80. It would have been much better for the government to have taken this step in 1964 when it would have given some room for controlled expansion but the maintenance of the pound's value was regarded as a matter of confidence and prestige, especially as it was Labour which had devalued in 1949.

By this time, it had become very evident that Britain's competitive position in the world economy was deteriorating and that this was an important factor in the tendency for imports to rise faster than exports as soon as the economy was allowed to expand a little. It was not that British industry was unable to produce more goods and even increase productivity significantly. The overall rate of increase in manufacturing production of some 3½% p.a. in this period was higher than for a very long time. By 1967 output per person was 47% above 1950 even with the shorter hours worked. The brutal fact was that our European and Japanese competitors were moving ahead even faster, albeit in some cases from lower base levels. Germany in particular had growth rates about twice as high as the UK.

It is not easy to be dogmatic as to the reasons for this divergence. Some part of it must be associated with conservative management and conservative trade unions and also to the associated deficiencies in British education and training. The low social and cultural standing in the UK of manufacturing industry as an occupation, as well as an object of investment, still remained a major handicap. In any event it was becoming ever clearer that to some extent low comparative productivity was related to the capital equipment of industry being poorer in the UK and that this was associated with a low rate of investment – some 30 to 40% below that of Germany and Japan. This is turn was partly historical in its causes but was hardly surprising in view of the 'stop-go' action of governments which clearly disrupted the steady expansion necessary to establish confidence as well as the profitability which stimulates new investment.

Indeed it really would have been quite astonishing if British industry had staged a miraculous renaissance during the period when governments were so often taking drastic measures to reduce not only consumption but also investment. The latter objective was quite explicit at the time of the Korean war when private industrial investment was seen as competing for the military equipment the government was planning to supply. More generally, high interest rates must be expected, if not designed, to deter new investment. British policy was always of a short-sighted character to deal with short-term problems. Other countries also had economic perturbations but some of them were already working on higher trend lines drawn by purposive governments far less inclined to leave everything to market forces especially market forces conditioned by short-term panic measures.

The loss of domestic production caused by each application of the brakes in the UK was itself substantial and quite disproportionate to the amounts of money which were crucial for the balance of payments. Even with a modest measure of selectivity in the precise economic measures, deflation was and remains a very blunt weapon for fine tuning. For deep-rooted problems it may or may not be a cure but it is always vastly expensive.

But perhaps the most extraordinary aspect of the period of the 1950s and the 1960s was that the balance of payments was continuously handicapped also by the drain of money abroad from the considerable private export of capital as well as government expenditure. These hang-overs from the period of imperial greatness and industrial leadership clearly constituted crippling burdens on an economy staggering from one balance of payments crisis to another. Lack of realism on the part of governments was matched by lack of interest in financial circles in investment in industry, so different from Germany, for instance.

There are various measures of the effects of all these factors on the comparative position of the UK. British export prices, despite wages being quite low in relation to those in the principal competing countries and annual pay increases no higher, rose about 15% above the general competitive world level in ten years or so. The British share of world trade in manufactures fell by half between 1950 and 1966 to 13%. In certain circumstances a reduction in share in world trade when the economic world was growing might not have been too serious but these circumstances certainly did not obtain in the 1960s. The basic fact was that the country's productivity was not rising fast enough to compete with Europe and the Far East, nor to pay wages which allowed a continuous modest real increase.

The stresses which all this imposed on the labour market became in fact of increasing concern during the 1960s. In 1961 the Chancellor of the Exchequer ordered a 'pay pause' for six months. In 1964 the new Labour government established the National Board for Prices and Incomes on the basis that the planned economic expansion would require some containment of wages in particular. In fact the whole experiment developed into a disaster when the supposed flexible control instrument had to be applied to help to deflate the economy in a period of crisis in the balance of payments. The original concept of voluntary agreement with the Trade Unions was diverted into a statutory control of wages and prices before it too was abandoned after devaluation of sterling in 1967. By 1969 there was a veritable explosion of pay increases. But for nearly twenty years inflation had been no more than the 2 to 3% level common to many countries.

Before we consider the 1970s with their very special additional problems, it is appropriate to recognise the magnitude of the changes which the British economy had achieved – as well as endured – in the post-war period. Consider first, the trade figures. Exports, despite the disappointment by comparison with other countries, had risen almost threefold in volume by 1970 compared with pre-war and had doubled even since 1950. By 1938 the share of exports in

Gross Domestic Product had fallen to 11%; it rose to 20% by 1950, fell to 15.5% by 1965 and rose again to 18% in 1970 and back to 20.5% by 1975 when imports were at 24% of Gross Expenditure. The terms of trade, a major source of added burdens in the early post-war period as world food and material prices rose, recovered by 20% in Britain's favour from 1955 to 1965 and 1970, back to the more comfortable pre-war level.

No doubt this late beneficial movement helped somewhat to improve living standards but, quite apart from foreign trade matters, it is not surprising that the striking increase in production resulted in a similar increase in real wages of manual workers by some 50% from 1950 to the late 1960s reaching about two and a half times the pre-war level. Other classes probably benefited similarly although it is difficult to be sure. What is impossible to dispute is that the lot of working people was immeasurably improved by the removal of mass unemployment as a constant threat – still less than 3% at the end of the period – and by the provision of welfare services including the National Health Service. Primary poverty had almost gone.

It was in this period of course that, with basic needs at last safely covered, personal expenditure was able to extend to the consumer durables such as television sets as well as a variety of electrical appliances and most spectacularly to motor cars. The Affluent Society had almost arrived.

So what was the legacy that the 1950s and 1960s bequeathed to the 1970s? Wages were rising rather fast as if a log jam had been removed but following the 1967 devaluation the trade balance was in reasonably good shape. On a longer-term view, the economy had been transformed since the war, with penury changed almost to comfort. But there was a major lurking vulnerability to foreign trade as well as to inflation. It had become worth reflecting what this international trade was all about. Was it all worth while? Did we really need to be troubled by balance of payments crises? If we had simply been prepared to produce goods for our own requirements, could we not have achieved greater and more sustained expansion? Instead of raising living standards by 50% in two decades, could we not have doubled them?

Then second thoughts might set in, perhaps about

international specialisation in various products, a beloved theory of the economists. But in the real world it seemed to be all a matter of competition between manufacturers in different countries making similar goods. With international cartels there might not even be much competition. But this also was a distraction from the real truth. Competition did exist, often all too uncomfortably, but with lower and lower transport costs and tariffs, was it all much more than the leading countries taking in each other's laundry?

After all, it was all very well for Britain to have 30–40% of her economy dependent on foreign trade in the balmy days of the nineteenth century when she commanded not only the seas, but also the trade routes, the colonies, the sterling area and all the other territories prepared to pay tribute and cheap food. But did it all really make sense in the mid twentieth century when the rest of the world seemed to be conspiring to make life difficult for a small country, fount of Western civilisation and industrialisation as it had been, but now comfortably backward in terms of economics, mass production, technological development and general educational levels?

We ask these questions as an interim comment on the stage of history at which we have arrived as well as a warning as to what is to come.

But stop a moment. Our readers must already be saying that we have to have a vast export business to pay for all those essential imports. Well, yes, but how much is essential? A lot of raw materials probably but perhaps not as much as you might expect – after all foreign trade had been down, in 1938, nearly to a single figure percentage of GDP. And as for food, well with a controlled market, domestic production of home consumption of the major products rose dramatically –

(%s.)	1938	1970	1980	1987
Wheat	23	41	77	125 (Yes we had some for export!)
Barley	46	90	114	145
Beef	49	73	89	97
Butter	9	13	51	106
Sugar	18	25	48	59
Cheese	24	43	72	68
Eggs	61	99	99	98

The Ministry of Agriculture figures for total food self-sufficiency rose to a peak of 63% in 1984 falling back to 57% (provisional) in 1988. For indigenous-type food the peak figure for 1984 was 82.6% falling back to 73% in 1988. It is difficult to disentangle the causes of the fall-back but it could have had something to do with the workings of the Common Agricultural Policy of the EEC. In part it may well be attributable to increasing appetites (and purchasing power) for exotic foodstuffs since there was no obvious weakening of supply of the basic foodstuffs until 1988, a bad year for the UK harvests, although horticultural products did not quite keep pace with rising demand. In fact, the total trade position continued to improve after 1984 as export values grew from 39% of import values in 1978 to 52% in 1987, falling back to 46% in 1988.

In the next chapter there is some discussion of the effect of our joining the EEC in 1973 and specifically the expensive operation of the CAP. It should be noted that the self-sufficiency figures given in the above table for 1980 and 1987 reflect the effects of the CAP upon British agriculture. It is hard to say whether these high figures would have been attained if the old British controlled market had remained in operation. Probably not, since we would have continued to have access to cheaper food supplies from the Commonwealth and other countries. However the progress made even by 1970, at more modest cost, was quite remarkable. Further, in the thirty years 1950–80, total output approximately doubled in volume and the labour force was reduced by a third. British agriculture, already more efficient than farming in most other countries, had clearly been improved almost out of recognition in a controlled regime. So, if so much could be achieved in agriculture, what could we not do for manufacturing?

But it would wise to end this excursion into the world of food production on a cautionary note. Recent economies in the CAP brought a great reduction in British farm incomes by 1988 which was exacerbated by bad harvests. It is difficult to perceive where this change of fortune is going to lead, but it is surely conceivable that a depression in British agriculture will further reduce our self-sufficiency and the substantial benefit to the balance of payments of increased home food production. Indeed it now seems that the CAP is now encouraging or enforcing reductions in UK production in part counterbalanced by increased imports from Europe.

IX

From Consensus to Chaos: The 1970s

During the 1970s, consensus progressively disintegrated, not because of a single decisive watershed – that came only at the end of the decade – but rather because so many near-catastrophic phenomena occurred that it was difficult to have a consensus about anything.

To begin with, the Conservative government under Edward Heath, which was in power for less than four years from 1970 to 1974, having inherited a quite healthy economic situation with scope for some expansion of the economy, chose first to pursue a policy of disengagement, i.e. of no government involvement or interference, which was consistent with acquiescence in increasing unemployment – remember 'Selsdon Man'? Then as the number of jobless threatened to soar over the one million mark early in 1972, Heath realised he was heading for political disaster and policy was completely reversed in favour of an expansionist budget. This was successful in reducing unemployment by over 400,000 by 1974 but as shortages of labour, material and capacity developed, inflation again became a problem following a remarkable CBI price restraint initiative which had helped to bring the rate of price increase down from 10% in mid 1971 to 6% a year later, with a following wind in the shape of relatively weak import prices of materials and fuels.

In parallel with these developments, the Government introduced a scheme to remove controls on bank lending which was inevitably inflationary, although its likely effect was underestimated. This significant step towards a free market left only the rate of interest to control borrowing, but as the credit boom gained strength, Heath was reluctant to use this sole control and the boom got out of hand: the Barber era was a remarkable pre-run of the Lawson era, although not on so horrendous a scale.

In the meantime, prices and wages began to get out of hand. The miners secured a huge pay increase and attempts to achieve voluntary restraint through the TUC and CBI broke down. So a statutory prices and income policy was introduced in November 1973.

So many things were happening at once in this turbulent period that it is difficult to provide an orderly account. In fact, if it were orderly it would be out of the character with the times! There were in fact two major external shocks to the domestic economy which effectively moved from something of a crisis in 1973 towards something near chaos. Of these two external developments, one, the entry of the UK into the European Community, vigorously led by Edward Heath, was relatively slow to have its effect and we will return to it a little later. The other and more immediately horrendous happening was the first oil crisis, triggered by the Arab embargo, leading to a fourfold increase in oil prices.

In fairness to all concerned, including Heath, the acute severity of the impact of the oil crisis can hardly be overstressed. Its consequences were threefold. The most obvious was that it was directly inflationary in affecting the price of a vital material which soon raised costs over a wide area of the British and other Western economies. Secondly, and soon to be quite as noticeable, was the drastic effect on the balance of payments of the oil-importing countries, a swift worsening of the terms of trade which was soon costing the UK over £2½ billion a year.

But the worst consequence of all was that the sudden drain of wealth from the developed oil-importing countries to the Arab nations was seriously destabilising for the West. Until the Arab nations found ways of recirculating their wealth back into the world economy there was an inevitable widespread demand – deflationary movement as individual Western countries lost money and sought to correct price inflation and balance of payments deficits. These were world problems of a kind of which governments had had no previous experience and which could be compared only with those of a substantial war, not of course a major world war, but worse probably than those of the Korean War in the 1950–52 period.

Just to complicate matters further, the international financial scene had for the previous year or two been in a state of flux without precedent since the Second World War. As international movements of capital became larger and more volatile, the Bretton-Woods system of managed exchange rates began to break down in the early 1970s. Consistently with his new concern for expansion of the British economy, Heath tried to secure a reasonably low rate for sterling in the Smithsonian Stabilisation Agreement of December 1971, but having failed to do so, had little alternative in the Spring of 1972 to allowing the pound to float; the other major currencies followed suit not long after.

It is very clear, even from the foregoing very simplified account of the turbulent early 1970s, that economic policy had to deal with unprecedented and major strands of developments which were interwoven into a complex skein which was impossible to unravel or manage into an orderly pattern. It is certainly true that major policy mistakes were made by the British government, but in retrospect it is difficult not to feel some sympathy for Heath in that he was so soon faced with external blows of a very serious kind, of which the oil crisis was the most immediately damaging. In drawing comparisons between the UK's economic performance in the 1970s and its achievements, such as they were, in other decades, it is very necessary to make a major allowance for the severe and unwonted limitations imposed by these external trade and financial factors.

In any event, combination of internal and external factors led, not surprisingly, to a deterioration in the balance of payments from quite healthy surpluses of around £1 billion in each of 1970 and 1971 down to a deficit of well over £3 billion in 1974, of which over a half was attributable to the increased price of oil. Ironically, the oil crisis itself became a significant factor in the final events of the Conservative government. Having achieved some success with his wages policy, Heath finally lost his second war with the coal miners, putting the country on a three day week in the process. The argument that the high price of oil justified a higher output and value for coal was used to substantial effect by the miners in their claim for a large pay increase. In any event, Heath lost his appeal to the country by a narrow margin and let in a Labour government once more to pick up the pieces.

The new Wilson government never had a majority in parliament and had little power to do much more than survive. It did however, secure a voluntary pay agreement with the Trade Unions which was quite successful for some years, reducing inflation to a low point of 8% in 1978 from its peak of 26% in 1974/5. Despite horrendous turmoil in the world economy flowing from the oil crisis and the induced depression following it, the balance of payments was returned to a surplus of £1 billion in 1978, after absorbing deficits on oil account running at over £3 billion p.a. in the mid 70s tailing off to £2 billion in 1978 as North Sea Oil began to reduce the need for overseas purchases.

This quite substantial improvement by the Callaghan government (after Wilson resigned in 1976) was only achieved by a measure of deflation or moderate monetarism, with the assistance of an IMF loan and the wages control policy. Inevitably unemployment increased to over one million but was falling again in the last year before the 1979 General Election. Finally, Callaghan over-played his hand in trying to force inflation down even further and his wages policy disintegrated in the 1978–9 Winter of Discontent which effectively lost the election for Labour. The pent-up demand for pay increases, especially in the public services whose remuneration was always the easiest to control in crisis years, made some rise in inflation inevitable. By mid–1979 it was running at 10% and would have gone somewhat higher without new measures especially as the second major increase in world oil prices struck the Western countries. In fact of course the incoming Thatcher government adopted policies, including a near doubling of VAT, which sent total prices rocketing by over 20% again in 1980.

Considering that two unprecedented oil crises had been weathered, that the terms of trade had worsened by 20% in the 1970s and that a UK oil bonanza was just beginning, the final legacy of the consensus period was not by any means a poisoned chalice.

Much of the foregoing potted history of the 1970s is all too familiar to those who lived through it so recently. It may not therefore be appropriate to spell out all the detail. In any event it is not difficult to appreciate why many people looked for a new approach, without understanding much of the underlying developments.

There is however one major ingredient of the almost incredible economic mix of the 1970s which is of major significance for the thesis of this essay, and that is the consequence of Britain's entry into the EEC. For this was arguably, and much it was argued, the vital new approach to the country's economic problems. After all, we were in danger of becoming an isolated island in the great big modern world of large market blocks and mass production for mass markets. We had the choice, didn't we, of becoming the 51st state of the USA or joining the Community? Most important of all, exposure to this great new market would be just the stimulus British industry required. Could there be another such opportunity? There would be more and more trade and of course that had to be a good thing.

We are not here concerned with the political aspects of the EEC, but only the economic implications. In order to do this we must recall the long-standing requirements of Britain from foreign trade. Long ago in the nineteenth century, the country had become the workshop of the world and had grown a large population in these small islands which depended on foreign food and raw materials, as well as on a dominant position in world trade. Indeed, it was an essential feature of the whole system including the supporting structure of Imperial Preference, that Britain should buy food and materials from countries which needed the earnings to buy British manufactured exports. The loss of the dominant trade position of the UK had gradually reduced the real need for imports to counter-balance exports. Nevertheless, the increasing propensity of the British people, as they grew somewhat better off, to import more manufactured goods in addition to food and materials, had made the economy dependent on exporting to secure the balance of trade. But this access to foreign manufactured goods was something of a hard-won luxury rather than a real requirement. What remained most important was the opportunity to buy reasonably cheap food from all over the world and particularly under long-standing arrangements with the countries of the Commonwealth. This great benefit was perhaps the only significant reason for not further increasing the production of British agriculture, despite the considerable increase in the efficiency of British farms.

The basic interests of the major Common Market countries were quite different from those of Britain. To an important extent they were food producers, and relatively high-cost, inefficient, food producers in small farms. So the EEC was essentially an organisation designed to protect its agriculture, as well as being almost a free trade area for manufactured goods. In the latter field, in some countries, it encompassed industries many of which had long before surpassed most British firms in their equipment and efficiency.

So in joining the EEC, the UK was condemned to higher costs of food since the old southern hemisphere sources had to be progressively cut off in favour of the EEC farmers; and at the same time to the exposure of her industry to the relentless competition of powerful industrial rivals. It was quite astonishing to hear the propaganda about the new opportunities for British industry with never a mention of the more relevant opportunities for European industry to mop up the UK market. I well recall attending a public meeting in the early 1970s to hear a Cabinet Minister Mr John Davies, who happened to be a local MP, speak about entry into the EEC for which he was hugely enthusiastic. I stood up and pointed out that there were already relatively few barriers to international trade, particularly within Europe, and that the UK was already importing 25% of the cars we bought. I suggested to Mr Davies that if the remaining trade barriers were removed we might well find that 40 or 50% of our cars would be imported. Clearly neither Mr Davies nor most of the audience saw this as a likely possibility. But of course, it happened.

It cannot be emphasised too strongly that in free competition in free trade conditions, without any external interventions, the stronger, larger and more profitable companies or countries will almost always strengthen their position at the expense of their weaker competitors. Further, if the normal development of trade is disturbed by external shocks, even if these do not favour one competing group over another, this will generally improve the position of the strong compared with the weak, Any chance the latter have of building up their strength with new developments, new products and new methods, must depend on an extensive and extended plan which may well take many years to fructify. A major shock to the market, an oil crisis or world depression, for instance, will make it virtually impossible for such plans to succeed. It is the strong and profitable who survive in the storm and indeed take the opportunity to encroach on the preserves of the weak who are wilting.

There was in fact one important respect in which British industry started with a specific handicap on entering the EEC. The system of imperial preference had continued in substantial operation so that British purchases of relatively cheap food on long-term contracts with the Commonwealth countries was coupled with reduced import duties on British goods sold to many of these countries. In the meantime British exporters had developed long-standing trade links with the old Empire countries. This somewhat cosy system had been progressively modified since the 1930s as the developing countries perceived benefits from wider trading arrangements and many of them secured increasing political independence and freedom of operation. So although the special arrangements for food supplies to the UK tended to endure as being valuable to all parties, British exporters found their privileged position in Commonwealth markets being impaired by fewer and lower preferential import duties and also by a significant weakening of the close imperial family ties of trade. This secular change represented an important handicap to the growth of British trade in the post-war period.

Nevertheless, some significant trade benefits remained by the 1970s which were substantially lost as a result of entry into the EEC. Theoretically British exports secured almost a balancing benefit in that they could in future be sold to the EEC countries without paying import duties, but to secure much of this benefit involved a further restructuring of manufactured exports away from the old commercial links with the Commonwealth towards new customers with new requirements. Further, any benefit from this new market could, as we have noted, only be achieved in the face of fierce competition from better equipped and more efficient European companies who were also able more readily to invade the British market.

What many of us feared would be the result of entry into the Common Market was amply demonstrated by events. The following are the Department of Trade and Industry's figures for Visible Trade with the European Community on a Balance on Payments basis:-

(£m)	Exports	Imports	Visible Balance	Exports as % of Imports
1970	2,620	2,485	+ 135	105
1971	2,782	2,914	− 132	95
1972	3,122	3,664	− 542	85
1973	4,176	5,498	− 1322	76
1974	5,946	8,046	− 2100	74
1975	6,623	9,072	− 2449	73
1976	9,479	11,675	− 2196	81
1977	12,414	14,223	− 1809	87
1978	14,058	16,545	− 2487	85
1979	18,084	20,793	− 2709	87

The immediate impact of EEC entry in 1972 is very clear – a rapid deterioration of the UK position. There was some recovery in the Callaghan government years in the late 1970s, which continued into the early 1980s mainly because severe deflation in the UK reduced our ability to buy imports from anywhere. But by 1987 the trade gap was over £9 billion and the ratio of exports to imports down to 81% and in 1988 the deficit was over £13 billion, with an export ratio of 75% and with a trade deficit with Germany alone of some £7.5 billion.

Comment is superfluous, but all this was only part of the cost of joining the EEC. Everyone has heard of the government contributions to the EEC Budget, largely connected with the Common Agricultural Policy, which have provoked particularly bad tempered remonstrations in recent years. But far more serious than these was the increased cost of food itself. By acceding to the CAP in 1973 Britain was committed to raising food prices every year from 1973 to 1977 substantially above world prices. During the 1970s generally, EEC prices averaged about twice as much as world prices. The complex rules and regulations meant that all food of the major agricultural types brought by the British consumer have, since we joined the EEC, been over 20% higher in price than they would have been.

This was an enormous additional burden on the British

governments of the 1970s but mainly on the Wilson-Callaghan governments from 1974 to 1979.

But there was an even heavier cross to bear – the oil crisis. Britain had always had to import substantial quantities of oil as one of its necessary raw materials but the net cost had been bearable until 1974 when the real effect of the fourfold price increase imposed by OPEC was evident. The following are the DTI figures for the effect on the balance of payments.

£m			+ Surplus or – Deficit of Oil Trade	
1970	–	497	1980	+ 308
1971	–	691	1981	+ 3105
1972	–	666	1982	+ 4639
1973	–	943	1983	+ 6972
1974	–	3361	1984	+ 6932
1975	–	3062	1985	+ 8101
1976	–	3953	1986	+ 4056
1977	–	2775	1987	+ 4184
1978	–	1989	1988	+ 2344
1979	–	738		

The enormity of the problems bequeathed by the Heath government early in 1974 to the Labour government now becomes very evident. Of course the oil problem was not Heath's fault but the entry into the EEC was very much his responsibility as was the credit boom which inflamed and inflated the economy before the two international disasters struck.

For the Wilson–Callaghan government and indeed for all the inheritors of consensus the oil trade figures are particularly ironic. In view of the progress achieved by 1979 it seems possible that, despite all the weaknesses of the British economy and particularly British industry, a quite healthy position would have been established. Even as it was, the trade position was under fair control and offered a good position for making extremely profitable use of the oil bonanza from the North Sea which provided surpluses on oil account far bigger than any trade deficits which had ever been incurred or which would be incurred until 1988. The besetting problem which had beggared the British economy since

1945 was now about to be resolved for at least ten years, much longer if the bonanza was used sparingly.

In fact even a modest share of the £40 billion oil surplus achieved over the next ten years would have been enough to re-equip major sectors of British industry, to give them a real chance of competing in the modern world and to set the

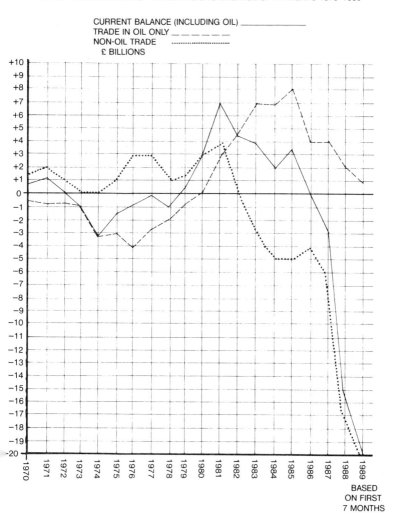

FIG 10.   CONTRIBUTION OF TRADE IN OIL TO BALANCE OF PAYMENTS 1970–1989

whole economy on the path of steady expansion which had
been so successfully followed by our major competitors,
especially Germany and Japan. This was the most wonderful
opportunity ever offered on a plate to an incoming British
government.

As we all now know, the opportunity was spurned in favour
of a dogma so sterile that far from being used to strengthen the
economy, the oil surplus was frittered away to the extent that
manufacturing industry was fractured with large sections of it
disappearing altogether, in many cases for ever, whilst the rest
was starved of investment to the point of negative net
additions to real capital over many years.

It will now be necessary to try to remedy these losses, not
with the protective shield of an oil surplus, but with the handicap of a vast trade deficit.

The terrible irony mentioned above is obviously that the
very commodity, oil, which caused the most serious problems
of the 1970s, was the one which offered economic redemption
in the 1980s but which was dissipated so that it would have
been better left under the sea. Yet the government which was
responsible for this overwhelming dereliction of policy has
been brazen enough to condemn all its predecessors for their
policy failures.

In the next chapter we shall observe in more detail the
nature and consequences of this perverse contrariness of
policy in the 1980s.

X

Monetarism and all that:
The Decline in Manufacturing

I well remember walking into the office the morning after the first budget following the Conservative election victory in 1979. Large reductions in personal income tax were to be offset by an increase in VAT from 8% to 15% and interest rates were sharply raised. Taking these changes together with the government's 'laissez-faire' policy on pay increases – they had long argued before the 1979 election that all the hassle about control of specific wage increases was unnecessary because control of money supply was sufficient – it seemed quite clear to me that the country was heading for a swift increase in the general price level from the 10% inflation rate of early 1979. Given the government's refusal to use any direct controls, it would therefore be necessary to apply savage restrictions on the money supply linked with large increases in interest rates. This in turn would raise the value of sterling. All these factors, high price inflation and wage increases, much higher interest rates, plus a rise in sterling, would inevitably mean disaster for British industry and unbelievable levels of unemployment.

So, when I arrived at the office that morning I said to anyone within earshot that by mid-1980 we would have 20% price inflation and two million unemployed and that we had better start considering now how to run our businesses with costs rising far more quickly than in other countries while sterling, instead of depreciating, which would have been the natural concomitant, would rise rapidly. Of course my forecasts were correct within a few months for 20% price inflation and two million unemployed, and the basic interest rate was at 17%. I do not take any particular credit for an astute appraisal – it seemed all so obvious to me. If it was not obvious to the government, one has to believe in an astonishing incompetence.

87

All that followed after 1980 was conditioned by the terrible errors of 1979. If the exchange rate of sterling is raised by 35% in a year or so and internal costs rise in the same period by 10–15% more than those in our competitor countries, the effect on British manufacturers who are substantially concerned with exporting, or competing with imports, is the same as if they had to pay a tax of some 50% on the prices of their products. So it was no wonder at all that vast sections of British industry went to the wall. I was myself responsible for running export businesses with a turnover of some £20 million per annum but fortunately we had a much larger amount of business in the UK.

The government, having deliberately taken the measures contributing to this situation, continued ostentatiously to wash its hands of the consequences, blaming them on market forces, North Sea oil and so on. The horror of inflation has for many years since then been the bogeyman against which government policy has been directed and the vehemence of the denunciations against inflation appears to have been partly inspired by the need to conceal that 22% inflation in 1980 was, to a substantial extent, the result of government policies. In practice, of course, the subsequent years saw the application of monetarist policies designed to bring down the rate of price inflation. But general deflationary measures of this kind constitute a very blunt weapon to reduce price inflation from over 20% to an acceptable 4 or 5%. This is particularly so if an over-strong pound is not only accepted but even welcomed because it keeps down import prices.

It is of course true that in 1979 to 1981 the rise in world oil prices was pushing up the general price level and was also tending to raise the value of sterling. But in these circumstances, the task of government was to moderate these changes, not to exacerbate them. Ever since that period, the justification for every act of economic policy has been the reduction of inflation. But the meaning of inflation has been completely confused. Not many years ago it was generally understood to mean the existence of excess demand which engendered a rise in prices and wages because supply could not be increased substantially or quickly.

However, in the 1970s and early 1980s, largely associated with the two great increases in oil prices, we experienced a

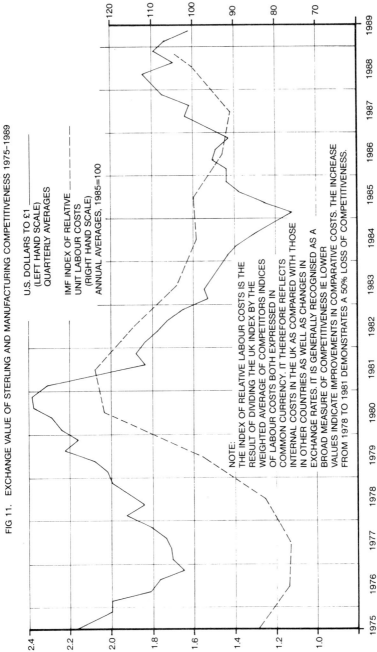

FIG 11. EXCHANGE VALUE OF STERLING AND MANUFACTURING COMPETITIVENESS 1975-1989

U.S. DOLLARS TO £1
(LEFT HAND SCALE)
QUARTERLY AVERAGES

IMF INDEX OF RELATIVE
UNIT LABOUR COSTS
(RIGHT HAND SCALE)
ANNUAL AVERAGES, 1985=100

NOTE:
THE INDEX OF RELATIVE LABOUR COSTS IS THE
RESULT OF DIVIDING THE UK INDEX BY THE
WEIGHTED AVERAGE OF COMPETITORS INDICES
OF LABOUR COSTS BOTH EXPRESSED IN
COMMON CURRENCY. IT THEREFORE REFLECTS
INTERNAL COSTS IN THE UK AS COMPARED WITH THOSE
IN OTHER COUNTRIES AS WELL AS CHANGES IN
EXCHANGE RATES. IT IS GENERALLY RECOGNISED AS A
BROAD MEASURE OF COMPETITIVENESS IE LOWER
VALUES INDICATE IMPROVEMENTS IN COMPARATIVE COSTS. THE INCREASE
FROM 1978 TO 1981 DEMONSTRATES A 50% LOSS OF COMPETITIVENESS.

a cost-push spiral of inflation which has posed quite unfamiliar problems. The principal method employed to overcome these problems has been old-fashioned deflation, however disguised in monetarist terms. But to break a strong cost-push spiral by deflation involves severe depression of the economy which happened quite widely in the world until the USA, in particular, reversed course under Reagan. In fact price inflation has been quite resistant to these deflationary policies which demonstrates their ineffectiveness in respect of their prime target despite involving a fearful price in terms of under-utilisation of resources. On the other hand the USA expanded its economy whilst maintaining low inflation and in so doing saved the rest of the world from worse deflation.

To understand something of the impact on British industry of the nightmare economics of 1979–80 it is instructive to read Sir Michael Edwardes' book *Back from the Brink*, which tells the story of his efforts to rescue British Leyland following his appointment by the Callaghan government. The British motor industry is inevitably exposed to the maximum extent to changes in the exchange rate coupled with the general price and cost level in the UK compared to other countries. British Leyland had to compete with foreign car makers over the whole range of its sales both at home and abroad.

By 1979 Edwardes had drawn up his basic plan for reorganising and re-equipping British Leyland, a project which was going to require additional government funding of some half a billion pounds. As sterling rose higher and higher during 1979 and 1980, Edwardes realised that his original plan was no longer viable. It was necessary to reduce more drastically still the level of operation planned for British Leyland and at the same time to double the funding required from the government. Edwardes vividly describes his strenuous effects to persuade the government and the Bank of England to change their economic policies but if anyone listened, no one would budge an inch.

It was in November 1980 that Edwardes made his famous speech to the CBI in Brighton when he stressed again that the pound was over-valued, interest rates were penurious and the whole issue was being aggravated by North Sea oil. At this point came the oft quoted (and misquoted) remark to the effect that if the Government did not have the wit and the imagination to reconcile our industrial needs with the fact of North sea oil, they would do better to 'leave the bloody stuff in the ground'.

In fact, as Edwardes himself made clear, it should have been possible to have our cake and eat it. The rate of exploitation of the oil should have been controlled as part of a general policy of keeping interest rates and the exchange rate at levels which enabled British industry to be competitive. In this situation, for the government to argue about leaving everything to market forces was quite pathetic.

The other extraordinary argument produced in those years was that the existence of substantial oil exports (or import-savings) was bound to mean that exports of manufactured goods would be to that extent reduced. This argument crystallises the totally static philosophy of monetarist economics. For why should we assume a fixed total level of exports? If the sterling exchange rate had been held down, it would have been possible to expand exports of manufactured goods *as well as* achieving substantial oil exports. The UK would then, on a distinctly higher level of total economic activity, have been able to afford a higher level of imports. The balance of payments must indeed balance, but the question is at what level.

It is a major aspect of the economic philosophy of the present government that the powers of government to achieve major shifts in the level of economic activity are very limited. But in 1979–81 a major downward movement in the level of the British economy was brought about in a very short space of time. A reversal of that process took a long time and ran into difficulties inherent in the process itself, as we shall see.

So what happened to British industry after the government's incredible errors of 1979–81? Let us look at some of the major sectors.

It is appropriate after our reference to Michael Edwardes to consider first the industrial sector, *Road Vehicles* which in 1988 incurred the largest trade deficit. In the years 1978–1981, exports and imports of road vehicles were roughly in balance at a little over £3 billion each, a sharp rise of imports of cars in 1979 not being sustained no doubt because of the depressed state of the economy in 1980 and 1981. However, as things picked up from 1982 onwards, with sterling still considerably over-valued, imports rose sharply to £4½ billion in 1982, £5¾ billion in 1983, £6 billion in 1984, nearly £7 billion in 1985, £8 billion in 1986 and £9 billion in 1987. Exports, on the other hand, were quite stagnant until the fall in sterling, down to $1.10 early in 1985, helped the industry to achieve almost £4 billion in each of 1985 and 1986, and even close to £5 billion in 1987. The most striking aspect of these figures is the sustained rise in imports after 1981 which was hardly affected by economic conditions in the UK or the sterling exchange rate. The trend was indeed quite remorseless and no one has cause for surprise at the approaching apocalyse of 1988. Already in both 1986 and 1987 there was a trade gap of some £4 billion well over 75% of which was in passenger cars.

So with a phenomenal credit boom in 1988 coupled with tax reductions and a rising value of sterling, it was hardly surprising that the total UK sales were about 10% higher and all the increase in supply came from imports. Export values were only slightly up while imports rocketed to well over £11 billion and the trade gap to over £6 billion. In the last half of 1988, the deficit was running at an annual rate approaching £7 billion and a similar level persisted in the first eight months of 1989.

Of course the deterioration in 1988 was particularly severe but if the short-term mistakes in economic policy had not been made it would seem clear that the worsening of the trade balance would only have been delayed – 1989 would have been as 1988 was. For it is extremely difficult to imagine how the trend can be halted and reversed. But reversed it must be, since there is no way the country can afford a deficit of £6–7 billion on motor vehicles alone. There is no intrinsic reason why we should have a deficit at all.

The tragic situation is that there is no longer a fully independent car producer in the UK. All the domestic suppliers are owned by, or linked with foreign companies. So we have completely lost control over the situation. One month Ford say they are going to increase the proportion of their UK sales they make in this country. The next month they announce the transfer of Sierra production to Belgium. The Society of Motor Manufacturers and Traders has given up hope of any short-term improvement.

The only real hope, it seems, is that the Japanese will decide to invest more in car manufacture in the UK although this may not be readily acceptable to the EEC. To what abysmal depths have we sunk when the Prime Minister beseeches Toyota to put a new assembly plant in Britain and rejoices in triumph when they agree?

Even if the motor vehicle industry was the only one in serious deficit it would hardly be possible to contemplate accepting the present situation, which is likely to continue to deteriorate if the UK economy expands at a significant rate. In fact most other industries have gone increasingly into deficit over the last ten years.

Our old friend the *Textiles* industry, long reduced to a shadow of its former self, actually maintained a surplus of exports over imports until 1978 and modest deficits of £0.2 to £0.3 billion p.a. were incurred until 1981 when things began to go badly worse with a deficit of over £0.6 million which steadily increased to £1.2 billion in 1984 and £1.7 billion in 1988. For the first half of 1989 there was a small improvement in exports.

The related *Clothing & Footwear Industry* has somewhat surprisingly been in deficit for a long time, at least through the 1970s and 1980s, with a steady worsening of the out-turn. The Department of Trade and Industry figures for imports as a proportion of the total of home consumption increased from 26% in 1978 to 36% by 1984, falling a little for the next two years only to rise to 39% in 1987 and 1988 when the deficit of exports below imports reached £2.6 billion. In the first half of 1989 there was a further slight deterioration.

A 1989 report contrasts the more modern and efficient equipment in the clothing industry in Germany with that in Britain, coupled with the more effective use of automation, particularly in production planning. The quality of the German clothing is much higher, commanding prices for exported women's dresses, for instance, two and a half times the average for British dresses made to simpler designs in longer runs. The report states that the overwhelming reason for the Germans' success lies in the high standards of training and resulting levels of skill, with ten times as many people taking the basic training programme!

In *Paper, Printing and Publishing*, import penetration increased only comparatively slowly from 19% in 1978 to 22% in 1987

and 1988 with the trade deficit widening from £1.3 billion to
£3.0 billion in 1988.

The DTI classifications of *Metal Manufactures, Non-Ferrous
Metals* and *Iron and Steel* tell a more complex story. The
category *Metal Manufacture* was strongly in surplus with
exports 70–100% above imports until the period 1978–82
when they were around 50% up, falling thereafter and going
into deficit in 1985 and ending £0.6 billion in the red in 1988.
Non-Ferrous Metals were always in deficit in the 1970s and 1980s
to the extent of some hundreds of million pounds p.a. with
the import proportion rising in recent years, from 28% in
1983 to 39% in 1987. In this category there was, somewhat
exceptionally, a particularly severe deterioration in 1988 with
the deficit doubling to over £0.8 billion. *Iron & Steel*, on the
other hand, after being in surplus through the 1970s,
achieved no more than parity in 1977–1979, falling badly in
1980, improving a little thereafter to achieve surpluses in
1985–1987 only to fall back to parity in 1988. In this industry
there was a significant increase in exports from 1984–85
onwards, but imports surged in 1988.

In the fields of *Data Processing Equipment, Domestic Electrical
Appliances* and *Electronic Equipment* the story is one of fairly continuous piling-up of deficits in the 1980s starting from very
low figures of £0.1-£0.2 billion and reaching 1988 figures of
£1.0 billion, £0.9 billion and £1.7 billion respectively. Within
these figures is the crucial modern field of *Information Technology*, which is difficult to define precisely. It has grown five fold
in the last ten years and, on a trade definition which is still less
than comprehensive, recorded a deficit of £2.23 billion in
1987, rising to £2.77 billion in the first nine months of
1988.

In *Timber and Wooden Furniture* there was a slow increase in
import penetration from 27% in 1978 to 31% in 1987, with the
trade deficit rising from £1.15 in 1978 to £2.5 billion by 1988.
A 1987 report on the kitchen furniture industries in Britain
and W. Germany found a productivity gap in favour of the latter of 50–60%. Typically, the higher-quality goods are imported into Britain, mainly from Germany. The heavy machinery
used in Britain is entirely imported, mainly from Germany
and Italy. Automation and machinery is much more effectively used in Germany where production planning and

timetabling is much more thoroughly done by highly experienced personnel. The following passage from the conclusions of this report needs to be quoted in full:

'The net effect of these technological and organisational differences was that the typical German and typical British firms visited were visibly of different calibre. Both had access on international markets to the same selection of modern machinery but the qualifications of those employed were entirely different. 90% of all German employees had vocational qualifications based on a three year apprenticeship type course followed by qualifying examinations; in Britain only 10% came near to being in that category. . . . It was with the help of a thoroughly qualified workforce that advanced machinery and operation methods were put into smooth operation and fully exploited. Our YTS scheme caters for an immense number of trainees, but the initial educational qualifications of the trainees and the vocational standards aimed for under the scheme are much below those current in Germany. . . .'

The *Chemical Industry* remained a comparative success story with surpluses all through but even here import penetration rose from 28% in 1978 to 43% in 1987, so that the 1988 surplus of £2 billion was no higher, in money terms, than those of 1980 and 1981 when the price level was very much lower.

There was however, one big success story. In *Aerospace Equipment* the 1978 surplus of £0.2 billion rose to £1.7 billion in 1988. The British industry is of course mainly in the hands of British Aerospace which has been successful in improving efficiency and reducing costs. Even so it has had great difficulty in making profits at recent exchange rates, with dollar revenues from civil aircraft sales not meeting the costs of manufacture in sterling terms. Its principal hope of improving profits stems from the vast Saudi Arabian purchase of military aircraft.

The following table summarises the surpluses and deficits in some principal industrial categories in 1988 with the percentage import penetration figures for the same year.

Category	Deficit (−) or Surplus (+) 1988 £bn	Import Penetration 1988 %
Road Vehicles	− 6.40	48
Textiles	− 1.70	48
Clothing & Footwear	− 2.00	39
Timber & Wooden Furniture	− 2.50	31
Paper, Printing & Publishing	− 3.00	22
Rubber & Plastics	+ 0.75	27
*Electrical & Electronic Equipment	− 3.00	49
Mechanical Machinery	+ 0.50	40
Chemicals	+ 2.00	41
Non-Ferrous Metals	− 0.90	39
Iron & Steel	+ 0.10	25
Metal Manufacturers	− 0.50	19
#Aerospace Manufacture	+ 2.5	63

* Including Data Processing Equipment and Domestic Electrical Appliances.

The import penetration in this case is somewhat misleading since exports substantially exceed imports.

A point of major importance is that, in all the main categories of trade, without exception, the figures for 1988 represent the effect of long-established trends with only minor ripples around 1985–86. There are virtually no sudden reversals of trend. In a few cases, however, notably Road Vehicles and Non-Ferrous Metals, there was a sharp acceleration of trend in 1988. This scenario is consistent with the total picture for manufacturing industry:-

(£m)	Excess (+) or Deficit (−) of Exports over imports	Exports as % of Imports
1981	+ 4,495	115
1982	+ 2,092	106
1983	− 2,715	94
1984	− 4,417	91
1985	− 3,623	94
1986	− 6,052	90
1987	− 7,828	89
1988	− 14,897	81
1989 (based on first nine months)	− 17,320	81

Clearly 1985 saw a temporary improvement related to the low value of sterling. In the absence of the excessive credit boom and tax reduction in 1988, the deficit in that year might have been expected to be about £9-10 billion, serious enough on any reckoning. The overall current deficit would have been similar since the other items roughly cancel out.

It is interesting to note that the volume of imports of manufactured goods more than doubled by 1988 from the average of 1978–80 while the volume of exports increased by 30%.

The following table summarises the major categories of trade other than manufactured goods, showing their deficits (-) or surpluses (+) in 1988 and the first nine months of 1989 (annual rate).

£bn	1987	1988	1989
Food, Beverages and tobacco	− 4.0	− 4.4	− 4.1
Basic Materials	− 3.0	− 3.3	− 4.0
Fuels (Non-oil)	− 1.3	− 1.2	− 1.5
	− 8.3	− 8.9	− 9.6
Oil Trade	+ 4.2	+ 2.8	+ 0.9
Invisibles (Net)	+ 7.3	+ 6.2	+ 4.3
	+ 11.5	+ 8.5	+ 5.2

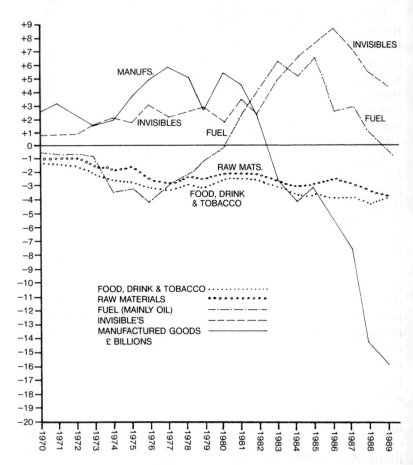

FIG 12. PRINCIPAL COMPONENTS OF BALANCE OF PAYMENTS 1970–1989

The figures show that the oil surplus and the net invisibles are progressively failing to pay for net imports of food, drink and tobacco plus basic raw materials. In order to achieve a trade balance it is necessary to eliminate the manufacturing deficit running at an annual rate of £17–18 billion and to provide an extra margin of several £billion to cover net deficits on other items.

It therefore seems clear that in order to achieve an overall balance an improvement of some £20 billion per annum for trade in manufactured goods is required compared with the position operating at the end of 1988 and the first nine months of 1989.

It is difficult to see how major improvements can be made in the other sectors of the current balance – a greater production of manufactured goods will in fact call for an increase in imported *Basic Materials* and each extra 10% of 1988 imports would worsen the current balance by over £0.5 billion. After a steady reduction in the deficit in real terms up to 1980, there has been little change since then although there was something of a surge in 1988 continuing into the first half of 1989.

For the category *Food, Beverages and Tobacco*, the DTI *Review of External Trade Statistics* shows a considerable rise in exports in proportion to imports from 1970 to 1981 and slight fall since then, especially in 1988. The trade deficit decreased in real terms over a long period until the last few years. This category includes both basic agricultural products and manufactured foods and it is not easy from published figures to disentangle them accurately, but from the DTI publication *MQ10* which analyses overseas trade in terms of industries, it appears that the basic agricultural sector continued to improve its trade position right up to 1986 when the deficit was a little lower in money terms than in 1978 and 1979 but there was a sharp fall in exports in 1987 with a deficit of some £2 billion in that year, rising to £2½ billion in 1988 but falling somewhat in the early part of 1989. The food manufactures sector however, showed a modest worsening of its position from 1980 when exports were 60% of imports to a low point of 52% in 1984 with an improvement to 59% in 1987. There was a modest worsening of the position in 1988 followed by some improvement in the first part of 1989. Overall in this category there seems little prospect of a significant improvement in the near future except to the extent that deflation cuts demand below the 1988 level.

As far as *Invisible Trade* is concerned, the apparently popular belief in a great bonus to the balance of payments from earnings on the great export of capital in the last ten years has hardly been borne out. The fact is that there are also substantial transfers of profits from the UK especially from North Sea oil. In recent years, net UK income from foreign investments, after deducting payments to foreigners in respect of their investment in the UK has only been some £5 billion and appears to have fallen in 1989. The following table summarises the principal components of the 'Invisible' Account in recent years, showing annual deficits (+) or surpluses (+).

£ Million	1986	1987	1988	1989 (based on 1st half)
1. Travel	− 530	− 1020	− 2042	− 2484
2. Financial, Transport & other services	+ 6777	+ 6702	+ 6207	+ 6826
3. Interest, Profits & Dividends	+ 5364	+ 4987	+ 5619	+ 3262
4. Transfer payments (mainly government transfers including to and from the E C)	− 2181	− 3411	− 3575	− 3264
TOTALS	+ 9430	+ 7258	+ 6209	+ 4320

It will be noted that a substantial reason for the progressive reduction in net earnings is the growing deficit on Travel account which may be modified for the time being by the tendency of British people in 1989 to take more holidays in the UK and less overseas, but the general trend is towards an increasing deficit.

The Central Statistical Office has reported that the invisible overseas earnings of the City of London have fallen progressively from £9.7 billion in 1986 to £8.7.billion in 1987 and £7.4 billion in 1988. (These figures are included within items 2 and 3 in the above table). It appears that the City of London has lost something of its dominant position in international financial markets. This factor, together with the increasing deficit on Travel, largely explains the major deterioration in the Invisible Account in recent years. There would seem to be little prospect of an early reversal of the downward trend. The severity of the fall in the net balance of Interest Profits and Dividends in 1989 may well be attributable in part to the heavy interest payments being made on the short-term capital

inflows required to finance the deficits on the current balance
of payments and the long-term capital account – see Chapter
XI (P 121).

The following table summarises the major developments
since 1978. *Visible Non-Oil'* covers Manufactured Goods, Food
Beverages and Tobacco (which as explained above itself
includes manufactures) and fuels other than Oil.

(£bn)	Visible Non-oil	Oil	Invisibles	Total Balance
1978	+ 0.4	− 2.0	+ 2.6	+ 1.0
1979	− 2.7	− 0.7	+ 2.9	− 0.5
1980	+ 1.0	+ 0.3	+ 1.8	+ 3.1
1981	+ 0.1	+ 3.1	+ 3.4	+ 6.6
1982	− 2.7	+ 4.6	+ 2.7	+ 4.6
1983	− 8.5	+ 7.0	+ 5.3	+ 3.8
1984	− 12.1	+ 6.9	+ 7.1	+ 1.9
1985	− 11.2	+ 8.1	+ 6.3	+ 3.2
1986	− 13.4	+ 4.1	+ 9.4	0.0
1987	− 15.1	+ 4.2	+ 7.3	− 3.7
1988	− 23.6	+ 2.8	+ 6.2	− 14.6
1989 (1st half − annual rate)	− 24.8	+ 1.1	+ 4.3	− 19.3

These figures bring out the steady worsening of the non-oil
trade since 1980, apart from a brief respite in 1985 when
exports increased temporarily probably because of the low
value of sterling. The acceleration of the increase of the deficit
in 1988 was sharp but by no means surprising in view of the
expansion of the economy. What made it all worse was the fall
in the oil surplus since 1985 and in the invisible surplus since
1986. It can well be argued that the extent of the 1988
deterioration in the visible non-oil deficit was increased by the
credit boom but if half of this deterioration is regarded as
short-lived froth which can easily be blown away again, the
total situation would still be very serious and deteriorating.

The change in the oil position is of course mainly a consequence of the substantial fall in price coupled with lower production. There could however be some increase in the oil
surplus when current North Sea production problems are
overcome and provided the price level improves a little or at
any rate does not fall. Allowing for likely increased imports of

raw materials, it remains broadly true, therefore, that the manufacturing trade balance needs to improve by some £20 billion compared with the mid–1989 position. This represents over 4% of Gross Domestic Product, a formidable amount, even though the turn-round does not need to be made in one or two years.

If all the improvement were to be made by reducing manufacturing imports from the annual rate of £88 billion operating in the middle of 1989, it would require a reduction of 23%. If all the improvement were to come from exports, the increase would be over 26%. Both these possibilities represent most unlikely scenarios with factory capacities presently reported to be quite full and increased market shares very hard to come by. The recent increase in manufacturing investment has only just brought the real level back to the 1979 figure and there has been vast neglect in between.

Of course, any solution is likely to involve a mixture of increases in exports and reductions in imports, a judicious combination hardly likely to be developed without massive new policy initiatives. In both cases it will be necessary to recover market positions lost over a period of ten years and especially around 1980–81.

In assessing the possibilities of the necessary recovery in the position of manufacturing industry, account needs to be taken of the deterioration over the last ten years which is dramatically reflected in the following figures for total output and gross fixed investment in manufacturing:-

	Total output index (1980 = 100)	Gross fixed investment (1980 prices)
1978	109.7	7,221
79	109.5	7,496
80	100	6,478
81	94	4,865
82	94.2	4,704
83	96.9	4,780
84	100.8	5,750
85	103.7	6,425
86	104.7	6,329
87	109.4	6,835
88	117.1	7,612

FIG 13.   INVESTMENT AND OUTPUT IN MANUFACTURING INDUSTRY 1978-1987

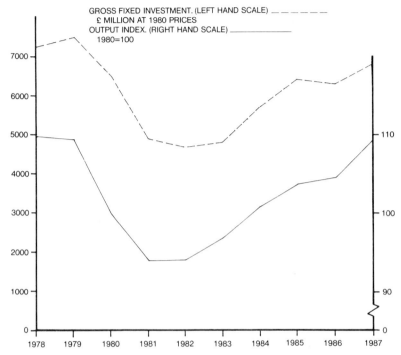

GROSS FIXED INVESTMENT. (LEFT HAND SCALE) _ _ _ _ _ _
£ MILLION AT 1980 PRICES
OUTPUT INDEX. (RIGHT HAND SCALE) _____
1980=100

Even before this period, the UK investment figures had been well below those of the other major countries.

Current policies are centred on deflating the economy by raising interest rates and keeping sterling high, in the expectation that this will cut the demand for imports and, by reducing demand for home produced goods also, induce manufacturers to switch to exports. There is little reason to believe the latter will happen judging from past experience. If all or most of the correction were to come from cutting imports and if there were no incentives such as devaluation to cause discrimination against imports, a reduction of some 20% in the total demand for manufactured goods would need to be brought about, which would obviously be catastrophic for industry and for employment: 1979–81 all over again in fact.

Even without such a large reduction, some increase in unemployment seems to be inevitable. As a result of the

1979–81 deflation the official numbers of jobless increased from a little over one million to over three million. In the last year or two the official figure has come down to under two millions but almost half the extra jobs are of the part-time variety, many of them for women who move in and out of the labour force according to whether employment is going up or down. Whatever the arguments about details, there can be no doubt that several millions more people would like to work if it were reasonably possible. Obviously what is required is an increase of 20% over a period of a few years in manufacturing production, not a decrease. This would be appropriate to replace sufficient imports not only to abolish the trade deficit but also to provide the basis for some moderate continuing expansion of domestic consumption. It could also provide jobs for an extra million people. (Appendix II contains a fuller account of developments in employment and unemployment.)

One of the myths which has been propagated in recent years to excuse or mitigate the decline in manufacturing is that its place is being progressively taken over by the service industries. Clearly there has been some increase in employment in services partly because some of the unemployed are prepared to take jobs for low wages. But there has only been a small shift of consumers' expenditure from manufactures to services mainly because of the relative decline in the price of manufactures. Most people prefer to buy labour saving tools rather than hire people – we are not, hopefully, moving all the way back to Upstairs, Downstairs!

So the crucial fact remains that people want to buy far more manufactured goods than British industry is supplying and selling and if they receive any sizeable increase in income they go out and spend it on foreign electrical and electronic goods – and of course, motor cars.

A very large proportion of these foreign goods come from Japan and in recent years there has been a considerable tendency for Japanese companies to invest in manufacturing industry in the UK partly in order to establish production inside the EEC with an eye particularly on the free market after 1992. This trend is especially notable in the car industry with Toyota, Nissan and Honda all heavily involved. Given the parlous state of the domestic car industry, the development of large scale Japanese production, with its well engineered and popular models as well as its renowned management and efficiency, appears to many people to be the saving factor which will reverse the flood of imports, increase exports even and generally reduce the trade deficit.

Somewhat similar arguments could well be applied to some other UK industries and indeed in August 1989, the Nomura Research Institute, an arm of the very large Japanese investment company, published a report on the likely impact of Japanese investment in the UK entitled *A Return to a Trade Surplus?* This report suggested that Japanese investment into the UK could average as much as £6.6 billion a year for the next twenty years, resulting in extra production worth at least £16 billion in the year 2000, with a benefit to the trade balance of up to £13 billion p.a. Some of the press reviews of this report appeared to be grasping very hard at this large and seductive straw and tended to give the impression that we need not worry unduly about the UK balance of payments problem since Britain is such a wonderful country that the Japanese will come in their hordes and bale us all out!

There are a number of important points to be made about all this. In the first place, an examination of the report itself indicates that the figure of £13 billion potential benefit to the trade balance is just about at the top end of a range of possibilities some of which are not at all favourable. In any event there is the off-setting factor of the remission of profits to Japan which could reduce the net benefit to the current balance of payments to about £9 billion. But even this figure is dependent on the various favourable assumptions such as that –

(a)   the production from the new Japanese factories will not displace existing or planned production from the traditional companies in Britain; a scenario which is most unlikely to be anything like fully justified.

(b)   the example of improved productivity of the Japanese plants and the resultant extra competition will act as a great stimulus to greater efficiency in the rest of British industry which would not otherwise be achieved; a scenario difficult either to dispute or quantify, but surely a counsel of something approaching despair.

It has to be appreciated that unless assumptions along these lines are substantially justified, the effects of vast Japanese investment in the UK may well be negative on our balance of payments. The remission of profits is a considerable negative item. The tendency to buy both capital equipment and production components from Japan or other countries ('foreign sourcing') rather than from the UK will constitute a considerable trade burden. Above all perhaps, further damage to established UK car producers may well result.

In any event the prospect of increasing control over large sections of British industry resting in Japanese hands for the foreseeable future is hardly one which can command confidence, let alone pride, in British minds and hearts. Foreign companies may, as time goes on, find all kinds of reasons for changing their policies – moving production elsewhere, changing their purchasing sources, for instance – in directions which are by no means conducive to the health of the British economy. Indeed, can one really rule out the possibility that in some presently unforeseen days of international dispute or merely of specifically Japanese problems, that the Japanese government will be prepared to apply pressure on Britain by threatening to persuade Japanese companies to take steps inimical to our interest – or actually to take them? After all, we all know that close links exist between government and industry in Japan.

Further do we really have to rely on Japanese example to induce British industry to be more efficient? To believe that it is merely a question of example is to ignore the severe structural problems limiting our performance such as the British attitude to industrial management as a career. Above all it ignores the basic problem underlying our industrial potential which is beyond the power of even large foreign companies to solve i.e. the lack of a properly educated and technically trained workforce. Unless we can remove this major handicap, which will inevitably take a long time, we may well find that the flood of even Japanese investment will dry up. The Japanese seem to believe British labour is cheap but they may come to think it is dear at the price.

No, there are no easy solutions to our deep-seated problems. Leaving everything to the free market, even if this includes relying on the Japanese to come and take over, will not work. We need to take major and positive measures to earn our own salvation. The next chapter considers some of the issues.

The Nomura Institute study does not declare what level of trade deficit the UK might be expected to reach by the year 2000 either with or without the postulated level of Japanese investment in the country but it appears to expect considerable expansion of the economy which is likely, without major policy changes, to lead to a much larger deficit in the balance of payments than the £18–£19 billion likely in 1989. The Institute for International Economics of Washington DC has, however, published an assessment for 1992 based on trends up to 1987 as part of a study of the global impact of measures recommended, both in the USA and in other countries, to achieve the necessary reductions in trade imbalances including the deficits of the USA and the UK. Assuming an expansion of the European (including UK) economies of 2½% p.a., the UK balance of payments deficit is estimated at $76 billion (about £50 billion) for 1992, unless the appropriate remedial measures are taken including a depreciation of over 20% in sterling against the German mark compared with the mid-1989 level of a little over 3DM to £1.

The forecast of a deficit of £50 billion by 1992 is of course quite hypothetical since there is no chance of economic expansion in the UK proceeding at 2½% p.a. until then because the surging trade deficit would necessitate the economic brakes being applied even more fiercely than in the autumn of 1989. But whatever margin of error is allowed for such a forecast it does demonstrate the kind of prospect facing any attempt to resume a reasonable rate of expansion after a short period of restraint at a very low growth rate.

XI

Real Economics

Causes of Disequilibrium

Many efforts have been made to explain the reasons for high unemployment both in general terms and with particular reference to Britain in the 1980s. It would be inappropriate in this essay to try to compete with all the sophisticated works of the economists divided, at their broadest, into Keynesians and Monetarists. But unemployment remains a major scandal in Britain and constitutes a vital aspect of the whole economic problem of which the adverse balance of payments is another manifestation. It is therefore necessary to take some basic view of unemployment in order to discuss adequately the potential solution to the balance of payments problem. Further, it ought to be possible to consider these matters in fairly simple terms which ordinary intelligent people can understand.

If there is any doubt about the close linkage between the two problems, we should observe what has happened during the last ten years. There can now be no doubt that in the period 1979–82, large parts of UK industry were destroyed or damaged so that in 1989 they cannot supply British demand. Consequently, unemployment went over three million and is still around one and threequarter million (officially, but at least three million in terms of people wanting work), when further deflation is being prescribed because of the balance of payments deficit in manufactured goods and of inflation associated with capacity shortages and resource bottlenecks. So unemployment at two to three million is due to be increased again as part of the method of reducing the payments deficit and inflation. To those who have reviewed the economic history of Britain as summarised in the previous chapters of this essay the situation is all too familiar. Only this time it could well be graver than ever.

Both these major economic diseases, i.e. trade deficits and

unemployment, must therefore be regarded as severe symptoms of disequilibrium in our economic system. The question is therefore what causes such disequilibrium? The great division among economists (and therefore among politicians) is between those, on the one hand, who argue that the system would be self-adjusting if only governments would allow it to work freely with minimum interference and taxation, and those, on the other hand, who say that there are so many things which can go wrong (e.g. a shortage of investment) that there is no reason to expect any kind of stable equilibrium to be established, or that some kind of unsatisfactory equilibrium may emerge which grossly under-utilises available resources and particularly labour.

In recent years the former group have re-emerged most strongly as 'Monetarists' emphasising the overriding need to keep close control of the money supply as the necessary and indeed sufficient means of curing and preventing inflation. The latter group are still regarded basically as 'Keynesians' although there have been substantial modifications of the original doctrines of Keynes himself, so that the qualification 'reconstructed', among others, is sometimes applied to those who believe that monetarism is an over-simplified theory which takes insufficient account of the realities of the economic world.

In the main, the theorists of the former school have controlled British economic policy over virtually the whole of the last two centuries and specifically in the last ten years whereas the latter had some influence from 1945 to 1979, but there have of course been compromises all along the line. It would certainly be difficult to award victory to either school of thought.

However, there is surely one general observation which can hardly be disputed. Economic history graphically demonstrates the dynamic nature of the forces which have brought us to where we are now. There have been so many stresses operating from so many different directions, some economic, some political and some social that even if it were true that in some theoretical sense there was a tendency of the economic system to move towards a balanced situation with an optimal utilisation of resources, it is extremely hard to imagine how any kind of equilibrium could ever actually be attained yet alone maintained for more than a moment in time.

This has long been recognised, for instance, in respect of the agricultural economy. A series of bad harvests causes a great rise in prices for particular cereals. Extra resources are drawn into the future production of such crops. There is then a glut so that prices fall to a level which puts many farmers out of business, and so the cycle develops. It is not long before farming is regarded as too risky a business so it is starved of capital and possibly labour. The result of the whole process is that less food is produced at higher cost (and probably the 'wrong' kinds of food) than could have been achieved by steady development in a controlled market. Certainly this lesson was learnt long ago in Europe and caused the introduction of supported markets in the UK and in the EEC.

The same arguments apply on a world scale and explain the plight of many third world countries from whose impoverishment the developed world is of course not immune. Changes in the terms of trade may well lead to world depression, essentially because they are destabilising. Now it is possible for theoretical economists to argue that in the long run everything will work out for the best but, as Keynes said, in the long run we are all dead.

If we turn from the relatively simple and idyllic world of agriculture to the harsh realities of modern international capitalism, even more powerful unbalancing forces are at work. Quite apart from wars, oil embargoes, political revolutions, great technological innovations and so on, with which the history of the last hundred years is well endowed, there are changing cultural differences between various peoples and many other factors of a dynamic character determining the major conditions within which the economic system has to work.

To speak of ideal equilibria in this real world is to abstract from hard facts to the point of gross irrelevance. For many of the forces operating are anti-competitive and many are cumulative and non-reversible. In a particular industry, if there is not a cosy cartel, there is often a conflict situation in which one company seeks to dominate and control. Once in control it is extremely hard to dislodge it. A cumulative force often operates in a particular country where one area booms and another is depressed to the extent that it may take decades for the situation to be ameliorated. The same can happen to a whole country within a continent. Whatever natural economic forces tend to balance this situation, they take such a long time to operate that many other factors will probably have intervened in the meantime to distract the correcting motions. For millions of people caught in the trap there is disaster enough to ruin their lives. For the country concerned there is enormous waste of resources and lost production.

The principal obstacle to the theoretical operation of optimising forces is indeed the result of the time lags involved and the complex interaction of often conflicting and always interwoven movements. These considerations make prediction of the outcome of market forces extremely difficult, as witness the gross errors of all the experts about the 1988 UK balance of payments. But more than that, the involved uncertainties make it quite unrealistic to rely on the philosophy of 'letting the market decide'. This is not to argue that markets do not perform useful functions, but simply that our tools should not become our masters.

There may well be situations when a government has to decide where its country needs to go and take action to control or manage the markets accordingly. The classic Keynesian case was the economy stuck with high unemployment with no obvious prospect of getting out of the groove, in which case increased public investment was the recommended remedy which is still relevant in the 1980s. But there is a precise and powerful practical example in modern Japan where the government took the opportunity of a recent depression to spend vast sums of money on refurbishing the infrastructure, partly with a view to enabling industry to work more efficiently in future.

There can be little doubt that even if a particular country's economy is for the time being in a reasonably satisfactory situation for steady development, with high employment and low inflation, it can very quickly be knocked off course by some external shock. The oil crises of the 1970s constituted dramatic upheavals for the Western economies for which no experience had prepared them. Although the British economy in the 1970s still had significant problems, it may possibly have learnt to solve them tolerably well in due course – after all peace-time full employment had only been experienced for some twenty years, a very short time to learn to make it work. But the phenomenal rise in import prices multiplied the difficulties and sabotaged the learning process.

So there can be no question that violent shocks are destructive to the economic system whether they come from external forces or government policies. It is very easy to damage and destroy industry (or agriculture) but much more difficult to repair the damage. Whether or not it is direct government policy which causes the destruction, reconstruction needs positive government action if a basically privately-owned economic system is going to recover in an acceptable period without prolonged suffering for many people.

Vulnerability of UK

In the modern world in which international trade is so important and so easy it is particularly difficult for a single small country to work out its own salvation, buffeted as it is not only by the violence of trade winds but also by the unpredictable currency movements controlled (if that is the apt word) by both investors and speculators. In these modern conditions an advanced but small country needs a period of peace and quiet and some defence against the predators while it sorts itself out.

The UK today is in fact quite a small country. Even the 8% of world trade in manufactures to which it has been reduced is still more than its basic size warrants. What is much more relevant is that some 40% of the national income and expenditure is directly involved in international trade. The total value of imports, visible and invisible together, is some 40% of gross domestic expenditure. Moreover, there must be much other economic activity in the country which is indirectly dependent on the business directly related to foreign trade.

Thus it is quite impossible to treat Britain as an approximation to a closed economy. When all the econometric experts make those wonderfully detailed computer calculations with their various opinionated models, they are in fact making implicit assumptions about the varying impact of the rest of the world on the British economy. It is continuously amazing, in particular, that even small changes in this or that measure of the money supply can be expected to have quite precise effects on inflation, imports, exports etc, all moving on smooth curves. The multifarious, complex and variable processes by which these effects are transmitted inevitably mean that any correct prediction is more a matter of luck than calculation or even judgment.

The inquest on all the miscalculations of the forecasts of the economy for 1988 has made amusing reading. It appears that there was one pundit, described as a 'broad monetarist', most of whose figures were really quite accurate, and he was applauded in the *Financial Times* for this achievement. However, it was revealed that the one significant respect in which this expert's figures were awry was the balance of payments which showed an actual deficit some £8 billion greater than he had predicted. Now of course this crucial error would appear to indicate that the quite good out-turn of his assessment for the internal economy had a large element of luck about it, since the whole package really ought to fit together. Yet somehow the home economy had secured the benefit of some £8 billion of extra external resources compared with the computer model calculations. If this had not been so, much else would have been changed. Nevertheless, congratulations!

It is in respect of exports that the 'model' predictions seem most extraordinary. The basic official Treasury view, presumably supported by their own model, is that the squeeze on home spending will cause manufacturers to increase exports in place of home sales. Now, these models are supposed to be based on previous experience and it would be interesting to know just what are the precedents for what really looks like a triumph of hope over experience. It certainly did not happen in the early 1980s following the last great deflation.

The following table shows the official volume index for exports of manufactured goods in the crucial years (1985 = 100)

1978	89	1982	86
1979	89	1983	85
1980	88	1984	93
1981	85	1985	100

It was only when sterling fell in 1984 and 1985 that exports regained the 1979 level and went higher.

Without some specific measures being taken to help exports, it is extremely hard to imagine how they are going to increase at all quickly. One leading industrialist, quoted in the *Financial Times*, said in the spring of 1989 'It does not happen like that. It's not easy to increase exports, it takes a lot of time and effort. I expect we shall do what we did in 1980–81, reduce production, pull our horns in and sit it out'.

Of course what the company will be sitting out will include a over-valued pound sterling. In the early spring of 1988 Chancellor Lawson regarded 3DM as a proper value for the pound, but he later raised it 10% higher with increased interest rates.

Exporting is Difficult

The fact is that even with a reasonable exchange rate, exporting is difficult and requires much investment in market study, design, product development, market development, customer cultivation and sales effort. The late twentieth century is completely different from the mid-nineteenth century when exporting involved little more than increasing production of standard materials and selling them to countries with no production of their own or very inefficient production. Today our exporters have to compete in sophisticated product markets with industries from many countries who are better equipped and more efficient than British companies.

This latter sad situation had already developed long before the 1980s. So how much worse has it become in the last ten years for most of which much of British industry has been struggling to survive and has been badly starved of investment? Its weakness was both demonstrated and reinforced by the import penetration which increased so markedly. By 1983 when exports were still stagnant below their 1978 level, imports were already 35% higher than in 1979, and Britain became a deficit trader in manufactured goods.

Starting from a basically healthy economic situation and a competitive exchange rate, but with manufacturing capacity well-filled it would clearly take several years for major investment of money and effort in export businesses to bear fruit in terms of large increases in earnings of the order of 20 to 30%. Starting from a weak industrial base with an uncompetitive exchange rate it will take for ever – well for eight years, say, getting near the long run indeed.

In the early 1980s there was much discussion about the need for a lower exchange rate as a means of reducing unemployment by stimulating exports and restricting imports. The balance of payments was not of concern at this time since North Sea oil was flowing ever stronger. Today however the balance of payments argument has become absolutely vital whilst unemployment remains a major problem despite the largely cosmetic improvement of the figures in the last two years. What appears to have been lost sight of is that in the meantime the exchange rate did in fact fall from the level of $2.40 down almost to $1 early in 1985 and although it rose again thereafter, the enormous reduction laid the basis for some recovery of export business and employment. Now after allowing for the relatively high level of inflation in the UK we are in danger of moving to as disadvantageous a position as in the early 1980s.

In passing it may well be remarked that it is an interesting commentary on the management of the economy that the sterling exchange rate should fluctuate so wildly – for instance from $1.7 at the beginning of 1977, to $2.40 at the end of 1980, down to £1.08 early in 1985 and up again to over $1.80 late in 1988. Against the French franc, sterling was fluctuating around 9FF to £1 in 1979; it rose progressively to 12FF in the second half of 1983 and the author of this essay well remembers the hopelessness of trying to compete in a major field of export business with a French company with whom competition had previously resulted in a broadly equal share of a large market sector.

For a country with 40% or so of its economy closely related to foreign trade, it is hardly surprising that rational business decisions, particularly about investment, can ever be taken when out-turns, whether in exports or in home business exposed to imports, are so dependent on fluctuations of this magnitude over a period of eleven years. Such fluctuations are quite unprecedented and would have been viewed with horror not only in the years of the gold standard but also in the

Bretton Woods era and could not conceivably have been foreseen when the pound was floated in 1972, an act which was
expected to avoid pressures for sudden changes. If we are to
look forward to any significant trade improvement in the
future, we must surely aim for greater stability on the
exchanges. Otherwise we are asking exporters in particular to
take risks which no sane person would take with his own
money.

Implications of Devaluation

But if stability of sterling is desirable, a lower exchange rate is
essential. Quite apart from unemployment, it is one of the few
major areas of agreement between economists that a massive
trade imbalance requires an adjustment of the exchanges –
devaluation to correct a deficit, or revaluation, which really
means increasing value, for a surplus. The only alternatives,
equally unacceptable, are deflation for a deficit country, inflation for a surplus country.

The principal arguments against devaluation are that, first,
it moves the terms of trade against the country devaluing and,
secondly, that it raises the internal price level by increasing
import prices and allowing industry and trade unions to raise
prices and wages – i.e. it induces inflation.

Taking the latter point first, it is worth noting that the fall in
sterling from 1983 to 1985–86 did not lead to a great increase
in prices and wages until a vast credit boom stoked by income
tax reductions in 1988, had its inevitable consequence. The
planned reduction in sterling which is now necessary could
well be accompanied by reductions in indirect taxes and other
charges (such as electricity, gas and water prices) so as to limit
the impact of higher import prices on the general price level.
(As argued below, the impact will in any event be less than the
extent of the devaluation). Some measure of temporary
incomes and prices control may be necessary but could
possibly be avoided if the devaluation were accompanied by a
clear demonstration that stern and positive measures were
being taken to prevent its being the start of a rake's progress.
The most obvious means of raising the stakes and increasing
the chances of future stability would be to join the European

Monetary System. This step would, however, only be conceivably justified if it were accompanied by a whole constructive plan to put the UK on a new course. As a substitute for such a plan it would solve nothing and could be disastrous.

The other argument against devaluation, that it causes the terms of trade to deteriorate, has been the subject of more ill-informed comment than almost any other topic in economics. Let us consider it in the simplest possible terms. The act of devaluation itself initially changes nothing as far as foreign currency earnings of expenditure are concerned. Following a 10% reduction in the value of sterling, imports' costs will immediately rise by 10% in sterling terms but will not cost any more in foreign currency. Exports will earn the same amount of foreign currency and this will be worth 10% more in sterling. Result – no change.

Thereafter everything depends on a complex process of adjustment. Some importers may reduce sterling prices to maintain sales as demand falls in response to the initial increase in sterling prices, accepting less foreign currency, so clearly the total effect on sterling prices has to be an increase of less than 10%. For exports the matter is more in British control, the precise out-turn depending on two main factors – the degree of control available and the policies adopted in applying the control.

For major exports like large capital goods, heavy machinery, aircraft engines and Jaguar cars, for instance, the manufacturers and exporters sell direct to overseas customers and can precisely control the prices at which their products are offered. They can, if they wish, simply leave their prices unchanged in foreign currency terms, accepting the windfall of 10% extra sterling receipts and leaving their sales level unchanged. Only if they wish to increase their market share will they need to reduce foreign currency prices and accept a smaller sterling increase. This opportunity represents the vital option which devaluation buys.

Now it has to be recognised that not all exports can be controlled in this way. If foreigners can simply come and buy goods in the UK at the old sterling prices, the country loses 10% of the related foreign currency earnings; the obvious and extreme example relates to foreign tourists visiting the UK. But one wonders to what extent this necessity prevails over the whole range of UK exports. Moreover, one has to suspect that UK producers and exporters could exercise more control over their overseas prices if they were really well advised and addressed their minds fully to the opportunities. In any event it is obvious that the net effect of a 10% devalutation is not as high as a 10% loss of foreign currency earnings. The precise results, over varying periods of time, will depend on policies in respect of securing increased sales at lower foreign prices.

Thus the net effect of a 10% devaluation must be much less than 10% on the net foreign currency position. The out-turn may be considered either in sterling terms or foreign currency terms (but the two should not be mixed up as often happens when even experts discuss this topic). In sterling terms, import and export prices will both rise, by less than 10%. In foreign currency terms, import and export prices will both fall by less than 10%. It is certainly unlikely that the increases in sterling terms or the falls in foreign currency terms will break-even for imports and exports, but the difference will be much less than 10%.

Of course, these underlying effects will soon be obscured by the dynamics of the developments in a multitude of different trades. Clearly, however, the terms of trade effect is far less important than the potential effects on volumes of exports and imports. The great merit of devaluation is that it discriminates against imports and enables exports to be increased. Again, as with other measures, it will not be successful in either respect, unless it is accompanied by other changes to bring about the enormous turn around required to correct the current trade imbalance. It is a necessary but not a sufficient condition for success.

Exporting and Importing Capital and Technology

In comparison with a number of other developed countries, Britain has become something of an undeveloped country. Without significant production of many electronic goods, for instance, we do not have an effective and relevant technology to exploit in the short run. Without a fully domestic car producer, we do not have indigenous models of cars which can be exploited at home or abroad. In many fields such as these the time lags before we can produce goods which consumers want in sufficient quantities to raise total export sales by 20 to 30% or to replace imports, even at current trading levels without allowing for normal expansion, are difficult to estimate, but they will certainly be so long that we may never be able to reverse the descent into penury.

Of course we are already importing technology, designs and know how, particularly from the Japanese in cars for instance. We cannot be too proud about this. The Japanese have done very well by importing technology in the past as over the years MITI identified the fields where it was needed and then encouraged and assisted industry to acquire licences.

Further, we shall also need to import more capital, but for real long-term investment not in the form of hot money attracted and retained by high short-term interest rates. But it is surely possible to import both technology and capital without losing control over our own economy. The Japanese certainly have no intention of losing control over theirs. This means that we stop the take-over of British firms by foreign companies by permitting only licence agreements or partial shareholdings. If we do not, our process of revitalisation may well be sabotaged by foreign and international groups who have their own reasons for switching production elsewhere or for adopting pricing and purchasing strategies not in accordance with British interests.

Now of course it is objected that British companies are so busy taking over foreign companies that we cannot possibly object to foreigners taking over ours. But this argument is doubly flawed. In the first place the prospect of British industry becoming 100% owned by foreigners cannot possibly be offset by equal investment by Britain spread around many other countries. We cannot afford to lose control in this way. It is one thing effectively to lose sovereignty to a supra-national organisation like the EEC in which the UK is represented and which in the end of the day has to take responsibility for us as part of the whole. It is quite another fate to lose control to a faceless variety of foreign and international companies who, neither singly nor collectively, have any responsibility for what happens to the UK as a whole.

In any event, (and this is the second flaw in the reciprocity argument) it is extremely doubtful whether the export of capital from the UK is at all beneficial to the country. What we desperately need is more investment in the UK which, as stated already, requires the import of long term capital. We need this investment to produce goods in the UK to increase exports and to replace imports. We need it to create another two to three million jobs. We simply do not have capital to spare. The only sound basis for exporting capital is if we are generating an equivalent surplus on our balance of payments of which we are not in sight.

Historically, the export of capital from the UK has always tended to serve the interests of a small minority of moneyed people, and more recently the financial community, rather than those of the British economy and the British people, although some benefits to the latter can no doubt be identified.

It is true for instance that in the nineteenth century it was largely the export of capital which enabled British industry to dominate the world and it helped to open up new sources of food from which our people benefitted from around 1875 onwards, but much of the resources could have been better used at home. Nor should it be forgotten that investment overseas has helped future competition to beat us.

It is true also that the returns on overseas investment have constituted a quite comfortable cushion as protection against the trade deficits in which the UK has almost continuously indulged for over a century. But the obvious consequence of such a comfortable cushion has been that life has been taken too easily by British industry which has not had to be fully competitive. The cushion has in fact been more like a crutch with the aid of which we have stumbled along in the wake of our competitors in respect of expansion, investment and efficiency. If all that money which went abroad, even in the 1970s and 1980s, had been invested in the UK how much better off we would all be today.

On the simplest of calculations, returns on overseas investments are worth only the percentage of profit on the goods the investments generate. If the money is successfully invested in the UK the total value of the goods produced benefits the economy, particularly via the balance of payments, but also in efficiency and employment.

Long term investment overseas from the UK (direct plus port-folio) has, over the past ten years or so, exceeded long term investment in the UK from abroad by, on average, about 3% of GDP, equivalent today to well over £10 billion p.a. while in the first half of 1989, the rate appears to have more than doubled. On a normal operating basis an equivalent balance of payments surplus on current account would be required to finance such investment. Instead we have a deficit of some £20 billions. This means that 'hot' money has to be attracted into the UK by high interest rates to finance *both* the current and the capital deficit. This is clearly a highly dangerous situation. A change of sentiment could precipitate a sterling crisis with unpredictable consequences. In any event, it is extremely difficult to see how interest rates can be reduced without some correction to both capital and current account. On the other hand, without lower interest rates, and a lower value of sterling, it is going to be very difficult to restore investment in industry and to improve the current balance. These considerations would strongly indicate some means of discouraging the export of capital.

1992

In considering a plan for steering the UK ship in the next few years, we need to see clearly ahead to the hazards of 1992 which are appearing downstream like rapids over which we shall shortly hurtle if we do not quickly change course. It is almost beyond belief that the same arguments constructed in favour of our joining the EEC should now be repeated to support our accepting even freer trade when we are in an even weaker and more exposed position. There is already a very high level of trade within the EEC and it is extremely hard to envisage how even more can be economically effective. A bigger market is not likely to be better in itself and will tend to favour the creation of even larger industrial organisations, which in today's sophisticated businesses may well be less efficient as well as tending towards monopoly or oligopoly. Larger international companies will increasingly become laws unto themselves with, as we have already suggested, no concern for individual countries.

Increased specialisation of production within Europe is surely no more than a theoretical rationalisation of no real relevance or benefit in the advanced technologies of the modern age. What, pray, are the special lines in which Britain now has an advantage which she can increasingly exploit in an enlarged market?

It is really quite extraordinary that so many economists and politicians affirm their unwavering belief in the morality and efficiency of free trade. It all seems like a throw-back to the nineteenth century in very different conditions, a veritable triumph of hope and belief over experience as far as the British economy is concerned. History, including very recent history, has demonstrated that the British economy will get the worst of increased competition. Without quite new acquisitions of strength, resilience and enterprise by British manufacturing industry, there is a grave risk of further decline. Despite all the hype about a supply side revolution, there are no real signs of any large degree of improvement which will enhance the prospect on a substantial scale. Accelerating import penetration is the most obvious proof of the parlous position to which we have been brought.

So complete free trade within Europe is likely to complete the destruction of British industry with more and more of Britain becoming a depressed area in cumulative downward spiral. Our country is likely to become the sick man of Europe, dependent for its economic life on increasing transfusions of assistance from Brussels. Now, the present British government is wholly in favour of 1992 in respect of freer trade but wholly against the two conceivable methods of our surviving the fresh onslaught from the big industrial battalions who look likely to swallow whole what remains of British industry. One method would be for the government to take appropriate measures to prepare our industry for the strife, of which more later. Failing that, we would be better to join Europe as a full political member and then all those Europeans would just have to look after us, wouldn't they? As things stand we are in serious danger of getting the worst of all possible worlds.

It is a curious fact that the greatest competitive danger to the British economy in Europe has increasingly come from

Germany. Our trade deficit with that country in 1988 was £7.5 billion or 55% of our total deficit with the EEC. This is the culmination of our rivalry over more than a century. To listen to all the ideological advocates of unrestricted free trade one would have to believe that Germany was a paragon of all the free enterprise virtues. Yet in many different ways its industry is more heavily subsidised than that of other comparable countries without even counting the provision of a labour force which is highly educated and technologically trained to an extent which makes Britain's provisions ignominious in their inadequacy. Public provision in Germany is funded by high government expenditure involving high personal and corporate taxes. Credit and the money supply are closely controlled through the banking system in a manner which makes the British reliance on high interest rates look crudishly amateurish. The OECD complains bitterly of all kinds of economic restrictions in the country which has nevertheless organised itself, bringing together industry, banking and government, now as 100 years ago, to dominate the industrial scene in Europe matched in some ways only by Japan in the world. To preach about our overriding duty to remove microeconomic rigidities in order to compete with Germany's titanically efficient organisation and education is the nadir of irrelevance and hypocrisy.

Inflation, Wages, Productivity and Welfare

Before leaving the discussion of general economic themes we need to consider further the problem of inflation which some people would link with unemployment and the balance of payments as a major symptom of economic disease and disequilibrium.

At the time of writing this essay, in the summer of 1989, the government's economic policy is indeed obsessed with inflation. In the previous post-war period inflation became associated with full employment and there seemed little doubt that the problem developed as expectations of continuously rising real wages conflicted with the realities of 'stop-go' economic policies dictated by short term balance of payments considerations, which were designed partly to curb investment but mainly to cut consumption by reducing real wages after tax, for which unemployment was both method and cause.

Against this background, it is not too easy to understand what is causing the current increase in inflation, especially as there is still high unemployment in the country. Part of the reason may well stem from the structural situation of labour bottle-necks developing in particular industries and of course especially in the southern area of the country, But there is little evidence of inflationary wage increases of a kind which would be adduced as a cause rather than a consequence of price increases. On the whole it would seem to be more a matter of the credit boom with the addition of tax concessions, encouraging price increases and inflating profit margins. This would be consistent with the flood of imports also no doubt with higher margins as a higher sterling value has helped importers.

So the basic position is that, given high demand, the economy has tried to expand faster than production could readily increase, even allowing for the assistance of imports. In short, capacity has been inadequate because of the structural problems in industry including those of geography. Thus, in the short-term we have something more clearly a case of demand inflation than anything seen in this country for a very long time – certainly not since the Heath/Barber boom in the early 1970s.

However in the present situation it is clearer than ever before that there need not be a shortage of capacity and supply were it not for the gross waste of resources which has arisen because of deflation, greatly reduced industrial investment and destruction of capacity as well as virtual cessation of apprenticeships and other effective training. So even with an improved entrepreneurial attitude on the part of some managements, they simply do not have the tools to do the job.

The short-term remedy for the consequential inflation is therefore deflation in 1989 which unfortunately is seemingly inevitable to cancel the excesses of 1988. This remedy may well get rid of the superfluous froth on the economy, reduce inflation a little and even stop the balance of payments getting worse. What is really depressing is that there appears to be no prospect of resuming strong or even moderate growth without the whole cycle being repeated yet again with a worsening trade situation and further inflation. In the meantime there could well be a further wages battle and higher unemployment.

The only way in which all this can be avoided is for government to break the cycle by taking steps to raise the whole economy on to a higher level of investment, capacity and output, specifically in the manufacturing sector, with drastic action to remove bottle-necks particularly those arising from structural and geographical imbalances.

For the way to avoid inflation is to guide the economy into a continuing and reasonable level of expansion using a very high proportion of the available resources of the country in such a way that modest increases in real wages can be earned on a sustained basis and that awkward bottlenecks are avoided. Unit costs will then tend to fall even without technical advances. If this kind of scenario could be achieved there is little reason to suppose that unrealistic wage increases would be demanded or granted. If they were, the economic brakes would have to be applied, but they are being applied now anyway.

Of course the major bottleneck in all these repetitive situations over forty years has always been the balance of payments, and the government's measures to bring about a sea change in the economy must be directed to relieving this restriction, of which more in the next chapter.

There will be some critics who will say that fuller employment and continuing expansion will restrain increases in productivity. This fear is surely wide of the mark. The examples of the successes of other countries such as Germany and Japan clearly demonstrate the vital importance of expansion, involving high investment and general confidence. Even in Britain in the last ten years the real rises in productivity have occurred during the expansionary recovery from the depth of the recession of the early 1980s. No, there is no reason to be fearful. Indeed, the only hope for our economic future is sustained expansion which increases productivity as it raises confidence of both capital and labour. The people have to earn this future, but they deserve the chance.

Above all, the ordinary people deserve the opportunity to

live normal lives in a decent environment instead of being unemployed or continuously threatened with unemployment and existing in depressed areas where vandalism and crime are ever-present menaces. Much has been written recently about the rise in general standard of living over the last ten years which has undoubtedly been substantial even for those on average incomes but much greater for those in the higher salary ranges, particularly after allowing for tax reductions. But the principal debate has been about the bottom 20 to 30% of wage-earners or those living on benefits or pensions and many statistics have been bandied about by government spokesmen and those concerned with the welfare of the poor.

Some things we know for sure e.g. the old age pensioners have been restricted since 1980 to increases in line with inflation rather than average wages, so they have not become better off, especially when other social benefits have been pared away. The additional unemployed or those who have been unemployed for significant periods during the last ten years have hardly been better off. Moreover, unemployment has driven many people into poorly paid jobs. The disabled have not seen much change or, if they have, it has been for the worse and the same must be true for many people dependent on social benefits.

It is hard to avoid the general conclusion from all one sees, reads and hears, that about a third of the population have not seen any improvement in their conditions over the last ten years and that within this total there is a significant minority which has become even poorer and, increasingly, homeless. (Certainly very few houses are built these days.) Real poverty has returned for the first time for half a century.

Surely there is a strong case for judging a society by the condition of the bottom social and economic sector. A society which neglects its poorer people is sick and needs powerful remedies. High among the requirements are measures to reduce unemployment by utilising all our resources.

Economic Miracle or Economic Waste?

We do not need here to repeat much of the recent debate as to whether there has been an economic miracle in the last ten years. For some time now the truth about the temporarily concealed deficiencies of the UK economy have been becoming increasingly evident. The carefully selective comparisons drawn by government apologists with economic performance in recent decades have come to appear as transparent as they have been contrived. Even the most vaunted claims about manufacturing productivity increase, which take no account of the sections of industry which have disappeared, are now seen not to justify any significant improvement except by reference to the mid 1970s which, as we have noted, were beset by very special external blows.

It may well be agreed that it is more relevant to compare the 1980s with the 1930s as was done by Sir Donald MacDougall in his Keynes lecture to the British Academy in December 1988. I am grateful for his permission to reproduce the two charts one of which (Fig 15) compares GDP for the years 1929 to 1937 with the figures for 1979 to 1987; the other (Fig 14) compares unemployment figures for the same periods.

Taking the latter chart first, it shows that the 1930s cycle probably started from a higher rate of unemployment in 1929 but after rising steeply for two years, levelled off and then fell steadily back to about the 1929 rate in 1937. By contrast, unemployment in the 1980s, after rising relatively as much as in the 1930s, did not start falling until much later and in 1987 was still double the 1979 rate. The difference cannot be explained by movements in the workforce, which grew more slowly in the later period. So it would appear that productivity grew more rapidly in the 1980s than in the 1930s – for whatever reasons – which could have provided the opportunity for faster total growth.

However, the other chart shows that GDP fell roughly as much between 1979 and 1981 as it did between 1929 and 1931, recovering more slowly between 1981 and 1987. It may well be pointed out that GDP rose sharply again in 1988 but not in 1938 and that unemployment fell in 1988 but rose in 1938 before falling again in 1939 to well below the 1929 level – whereas it remains far above the 1979 rate in 1989 – probably twice as high on the same basis of calculations – see Appendix II.

But in any event, it has become very apparent that growth in 1988 was largely a false phenomenon which was not sustainable without rising inflation and a vast trade deficit. It has to

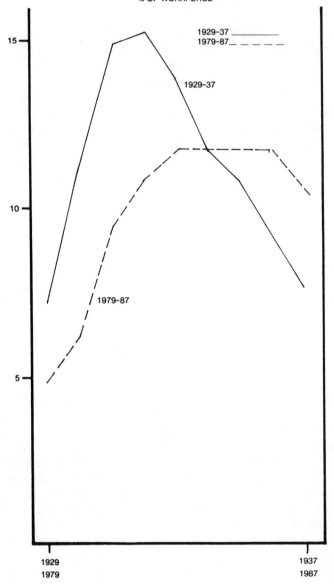

FIG 14. UNEMPLOYMENT 1929 TO 1937
COMPARED WITH 1979 TO 1987

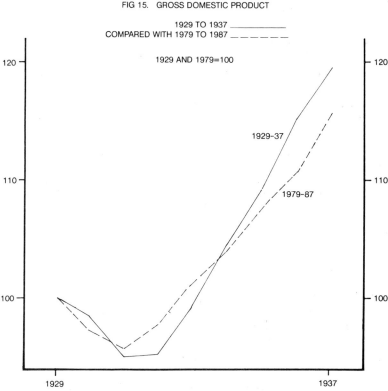

FIG 15.   GROSS DOMESTIC PRODUCT

1929 TO 1937 _____
COMPARED WITH 1979 TO 1987 _ _ _ _ _ _

1929 AND 1979=100

be considered also that the 1930s did not have the enormous uncovenanted benefit of North Sea oil.

Indeed with the great economic benefit of the oil in protecting the balance of payments it ought to have been possible in the 1980s to maintain a general rate of GDP growth of at least the 3% rate achieved over a quarter of a century during the derided consensus period up to 1973. Assuming this was achieved at a roughly level rate instead of following a vast slump with a fast splurge, the total additional wealth created over the ten years 1979 to 1988 compared with actual performance would have amounted almost to a complete year's GDP. On average, also, the national income could have been 10% higher, year by year, than the actual levels over the ten years.

Now even this would not have been an economic miracle, just reasonably good management. To achieve miracle status, one might suggest a standard of average GDP growth on a fairly steady basis of, say 4% p.a. – not too difficult with North Sea oil providing some 2% p.a. contribution to GDP as well as a firm support for the balance of payments. (After all a rate of 3.8% was realised over the seven years 1958 to 1965). The total addition to wealth over ten years compared with actual performance would then have been almost one and a half years GDP. On average the national income could have been almost 15% higher year by year than it actually was during the 1980s.

The reason why these startling figures are so different from those put about by the apologists for recent policies is that the latter usually and conveniently ignore the years 1979 to 1981 when the economy was plunged, quite gratuitously, into a recession which can be compared, since the Napoleonic era, only to that inflicted by mainly external forces in the 1929–31 period. The principal difference, this time, was that the damage was almost entirely self-inflicted.

If the economy is driven severely downwards for several years by drastic deflationary policies, it is not too difficult by reflationary and eventually inflationary policies to contrive a rapid expansion out of the trough which will last for a number of years, especially if the balance of payments is protected for the time being by a major external windfall, until the neglect of investment and training catches the country out.

XII

General Conclusions

What conclusions have we reached so far? First, we know that British manufacturing industry for a year from late 1988 was exporting goods at a rate of some £17–£18 billion p.a. less than importers were selling goods in the UK and that this imbalance, although accelerating in 1988, was the culmination of a trend beginning in 1980. In almost all industrial sectors import penetration has progressively increased. Secondly, the deficit on manufactured goods was masked over the period by the oil surplus but by 1988 this was reduced to so low a level that together with net invisible earnings it barely offset deficits on food and drink and raw materials. There is little prospect that this position will improve of its own accord and it may well continue to deteriorate. So, to be on the safe side, we need to plan for a turn round on manufacturing account of the order of £20 billion within a few years.

We know, too that the poor performance of British industry over the last ten years was hardly surprising since it had lagged behind that of powerful international competitors for about a century especially in the newer industries as they developed in each period, having been in the lead only during the greater part of the nineteenth century on a very narrow old industrial front. During the period of protection in the 1930s, many substantial companies were forged but operated mainly in the UK with little involvement in attacking the world markets.

Although the Second World War provided powerful stimulation, especially in the more advanced engineering fields, even the relative continuity of development in the UK worked against us when the devastated enemy countries in particular were able to rebuild from scratch on a modern, planned, efficient and expansionary basis.

After the post-war recovery had been secured by 1950, when a period of sustained growth could have provided the

131

basis for a new era, frequent balance of payments crises obliged governments to take deflationary measures which disrupted expansion and impaired confidence and the will to invest. Despite these setbacks, the third quarter of the century up to the early 1970s brought a great rise in the production of wealth, with real wages increasing by 50%, an improvement comparable only to that of the last quarter of the nineteenth century, when the great fall in world food prices resulted in the other marked step-change in the well-being of the British people. The third quarter of the twentieth century brought the other unprecedented benefit, war years apart, of full employment. These achievements should not be forgotten because industrial expansion was proceeding faster elsewhere but the fact of relatively low investment in industry and in people was ominous for the future.

The mid 1970s witnessed major fresh turbulence, substantially because of the oil crisis and the breakdown of the stability of the foreign exchanges but exacerbated by domestic policies and British entry into the EEC which raised food costs and involved industry in the need to redirect its export trade whilst exposed to even fiercer international competition.

Even so, by 1979, although inflation was a significant problem, it had been substantially reduced since 1974–75 and the balance of payments was under control with North Sea oil about to come pouring in. This situation offered a major opportunity to deal with the overriding problems which had beset the British economy through the century. The most obvious was the inadequate level of industrial investment. But equally important was the long-standing failure to provide the proper quantity and quality of education and training for the British people.

The gross neglect of provision for the working-class, only slowly remedied after 1945, had been long compounded by a woeful disregard for technical education linked to a bias towards the classics handed down from the public schools. The educated classes had been interested neither in technology nor manufacturing industry. In so far as the world of business beckoned, it drew them more in the direction of the City of London, than towards the industrial cities. However valuable international financial services were to the economy they could be no substitute for trade in manufactured goods and by the late 1980s their earnings were insufficient to pay for our now modest requirements for imports of food and raw materials, let alone a vast deficit in manufactured goods.

All these were the real underlying problems which needed to be resolved, or at least addressed, as the oil flowed in, producing huge tax revenues and major relief for the balance of payments. At this point in 1979, a change of government led to the application of an old policy of deflation, albeit disguised under a new name, as a cathartic remedy for industry's frailties. Thus was spurned the heaven-sent opportunity of re-equipping British industry and launching a long period of expansion unhindered by concern over the balance of payments. North Sea oil was worth over £40 billion in exports alone over the next ten years but probably twice as much counting the oil used in the UK which used to be imported. Yet some 30% of British industry disappeared altogether and much of the rest was crippled and its competitive strength gravely impaired. Investment in industry fell short even of the 1978–79 level by a cumulative total in excess of £15 billion. Exports stagnated, growing by a bare 30% in the decade, whilst imports doubled.

It will be observed that even if only a third or a quarter of the value of the oil had been devoted to additional industrial investment, some considerable inroads could have been made into past neglect on top of maintaining the level of 1978–79. Instead, the oil was wasted and, pace Sir Michael Edwardes, would indeed have been better left under the sea. For the government did not have the wit or the imagination to use it properly.

Of course much has been protested about the supply side revolution. It is undoubtedly true that a fair number of new and revitalised companies have risen from the ashes of British industry. But it is abundantly clear that they are relatively few and small in scale and do not add up to anything like a total replacement, even after so many years, of what was destroyed and damaged. Nor have the essential medium and large manufacturing firms in the staple industries been re-equipped with modern equipment and properly trained work forces. The trade figures after ten years clearly speak for themselves.

Even the much vaunted improvements in manufacturing

productivity do not appear, on close inspection, to be very notable. Over the last ten years the average annual increase is much the same as in previous decades and since a large section of the supposedly less efficient industry has been removed from the scene altogether, one would have expected a much bigger increase in what was left. We are left with the conclusion that in terms either of productivity or trade there has been no supply side miracle.

The history of the real economy as told in these pages clearly demonstrates the invalidity of the theoretical argument that market forces will naturally bring about an ideal or optimum resolution of economic problems. In practice governments cannot divorce themselves from national economics since they are inevitably involved in them in so many ways, not least in respect of external trade. Measures have to be taken to provide general control over the domestic economy, even if they go no further than control of the money supply, however that may be defined. These measures necessarily affect external trade also, particularly in relation to the exchange value of the currency. All kinds of external and internal shocks will distract orderly development, including actions of government. It is particularly easy for government action, as in 1979–82, to cause vast damage very quickly and drastically. To repair the damage, rebuild industry and recover lost market positions takes very much longer and, given the pressures of international competition and the tendency of the strong always to destroy the weak, may never be possible without very positive action from government.

It is therefore strongly argued that for British economy to recover so as to challenge the fierce competition from Western Europe and Japan it will be necessary for the British government to take on a directing, supporting and perhaps even protecting role similar to that which has brought such comparative success in Japan, Germany and France. The Japanese economic achievement has involved maintaining very effective barriers against imports of goods which they can produce themselves and the French are pretty good also at bending the rules in this respect.

In one important dictum traditional economics is surely correct, i.e. that a country that has a large balance of payments deficit must devalue its currency as the most effective general measure to discriminate against imports and to encourage its exports. This is a necessary although not a sufficient condition of success. If the exporting companies are properly advised about their pricing policies, this measure should not result in significantly worsening the country's terms of trade. In the past it has been successful for the UK, notably in 1949, 1967 and 1984. Its adverse effects on the internal price level can be mitigated by reductions in indirect taxes and prices of the major national utility monopolies, since a devaluation of 10% causes only a rise of some 2% in the internal price level over a year or two even if countervailing action is not taken.

We have also noted the vital importance of finding some means of discouraging the export of capital from the UK so that more finances are available for investment in industry at home. Equally, we should not allow our industry to be progressively taken over by foreigners who will increasingly be able to take decisions about investment and production in British industry. It is indeed a curious and sorry situation that we should have to look to foreigners to remedy some of the deficiencies of British investment.

One thing is for sure. Exporting is difficult, requiring much study and planning as well as much investment and energetic effort. Even with a more competitive level of sterling increasing exports will be a slow progress. To provide a stable basis of confidence to stimulate investment, it will be necessary not only to reduce the exchange value of sterling but also to ensure greater stability in the future. This will almost certainly involve joining the EMS at a competitive rate – well below 3DM to £1 – subject to certain safeguards, as mentioned below.

We should not allow current concerns about the balance of payments and inflation to cause us to forget that unemployment remains a great scourge which may well worsen as deflationary measures are taken. Structural problems and geography, exacerbated by government polices, have concentrated the people without jobs in the northern half of the country and although some initiatives have improved the position a little, major new measures will be required to bring unemployment down to an acceptable real level of well below one million. It would be most appropriate for measures to solve the balance of payments problem to make a major contribution also to reducing the numbers of jobless particularly in the more depressed areas.

But as we look forward, if that is the appropriate expression, to 1992, realism demands that we must be extremely apprehensive about the ability of the British economy to stand up to even more competition, even freer trade. Without some major new policies such as suggested in the preceding pages, disaster beckons. Even with all these measures, there must be doubts about success.

The basic fact is that the British economy looks just too vulnerable. One really has to wonder whether it will ever be possible, at least before the long run when we shall all be dead, for steady expansion of production to be maintained long enough for self-sustaining investment to be established which will not be continuously vulnerable to problems with the balance of payments. It is extremely difficult to be sure that a gradual process of improvement will not itself be disrupted well before sufficient momentum has been generated to ensure that it will be sustained in the medium term. To reduce this evident risk British industry requires to be moved on to a new higher level of robust strength and effective competitiveness so that it can reasonably expect to meet increasing challenges in overseas and home markets without continuously faltering.

But it is surely the home market which is crucial. It would be comforting to believe that most industrial companies can go out and enterprisingly attack foreign markets without a strong home base of business in the UK. But, as we have seen, export business is difficult, expensive and risky. Too much exposure to the risks involved leaves a company very vulnerable without a good and expanding business at home. There will always be a few exceptional cases of high risk operations which are successful but to expect the generality of companies to follow their example is not at all realistic.

The desperately vital fact is that in the last ten years, import penetration has bitten deep into virtually all sectors of industry. The DTI figure for the ratio of imports to home demand in respect of the whole of manufacturing industry rose from 26% in 1979 to 35% in 1987 and was at 36% by the beginning of 1989. If this lost ground was recovered, the current rate of trade deficit in manufactured goods would be eliminated. If it is not recovered, the exposure of the British economy to the vagaries of international trade and capital movements will be unbearable and will offer no real scope for future expansion.

There can really be little doubt that to recapture a large part of the home market should be a more practicable task than achieving an equivalent gain in exports. It is obviously far easier to know one's home customers and meet their requirements than to have to develop products and sell them overseas. There is a natural tendency for many British consumers to buy British if the products are available at the right price and of the right quality and the converse is true in other countries. The exchange rate risks are much less in trading at home.

Indeed, someone who has not been indoctrinated with the fashionable theories of free trade may well wonder whether it would be possible to mount a respectable case for a longer term aim of a much higher level of UK self-sufficiency, so that the whole economy could function on a steady expansionist level without always looking over its figurative shoulder at the rest of the world. Even agriculture could, if it were really organised to do so, produce more than the current level of some 60% of domestic food consumption. We would of course need to import substantial quantities of raw materials but we should have enough oil for our own consumption for the foreseeable future. The technological path of modern industry is so clearly mapped ahead that more is to be gained by effectively exploiting the available developments than by over-emphasis on the benefits of international specialisation and competition.

Inevitably an extreme policy of self-sufficiency would be denounced by all the economic pundits and apostles of free trade and international capital as well as by our competitor countries but it has at least as much logic to it as the opposite course of blindly entrusting our future to the international markets without greater industrial strength and better economic weapons than are presently in sight. Positive action of some magnitude needs to be taken to reverse the decline into depression which is now threatened.

In any event, a major movement to a high degree of self-sufficiency could only be a long term objective. What is more immediately relevant is that a major step should be taken along the path of reducing the dependence of the British economy on imports and short-term capital movements by ensuring that more of the goods the British people want to buy are produced at home. This is the most sure and certain way of correcting the balance of payments deficit on an enduring foundation and of giving British industry a sound home basis for future efforts to maintain and expand its export potential.

It may well be argued that this is easier said than done. Certainly it will require measures which are quite inconsistent with current (1989) government policy which relies almost entirely on maintaining a high rate of interest. This policy will undoubtedly restrain both consumption and investment and therefore, in turn, inflation and the trade deficit. By the autumn of 1989 it appears that the result so far is stabilisation of the economy with virtually no growth in national product and a marginal reduction in the trade deficit. There is a growing realisation that it will take several years of this degree of restraint to reduce the deficit to more manageable proportions – say to 50% of the 1988 level. The alternative will be even more deflationary measures so as to bring about a sharp reduction in national product and consumption. Either way, investment will be prejudiced and unemployment will rise.

The basic defect in this policy is that it is non-discriminatory. It involves using only one very blunt club to batter the economy into shape when what is really required is an array of more delicate and selective scalpels. There is therefore a high risk of doing so much damage that a further severe depression will leave the economy in even worse shape than in 1981 to recover its health.

The essential point is that to shift 4 to 5% of GDP into reducing imports or expanding exports is a monumental task, especially as the change has effectively to be brought about within the manufacturing sector. Put at its simplest, to reduce imports of manufactured goods by over 20% on a selective basis, involves reducing total consumption of such goods by less than 10%. On a non-selective basis it involves reducing consumption by over 20%. To the extent to which exports can be simultaneously increased, this penalty can be reduced but to achieve a tolerable balance of adjustments would indeed be an economic miracle.

The prospect is indeed daunting. Surely therefore we need to consider measures currently regarded as unthinkable. One obvious method of discriminating against imports and in favour of exports is, as we have already noted, to allow the exchange value of sterling to fall. But this is unlikely to be nearly enough. Some substantial and more specific measures need to be taken which will involve government in direct efforts to create new industrial capacity, particularly in the more depressed areas of the country.

New industrial centres need to be created to replace the old ones, centres of industrial excellence where a climate of cooperative national effort can develop with industrial companies, trade unions and government working together to achieve the paramount objective of replacing imports – and also increasing exports. In promoting and encouraging this kind of development, the government objective might well be to work so far as possible through private enterprise by offering financial incentives, tax concessions or even special grants. Cooperative arrangements between separate companies might well be encouraged. Joint ventures between private industry and government might well be necessary, In the last resort, direct government enterprises might be established.

It will be imperative to invest also in the necessary physical infrastructure and, most important of all, in the training of labour. Instead however of somewhat generalised training programmes, the new initiatives must be directed towards the specific industrial objectives of each area and each trade. There is an enormous lee way to be made up both in specialised industrial training and in the general level of education of the people as the reports mentioned in chapter X on the clothing and furniture industries conclusively prove.

Measures such as these would be essential in any event if the UK is to earn its living in the modern world and recover the potential to expand its economy without repeatedly being restrained by balance of payments problems and inflationary bottlenecks. The prospect of even freer trade and fiercer competition in 1992 only reinforces the compelling requirement to strengthen industry by stimulating investment, research and development and the training of workers, including managers.

Time is very short. Before it is too late we need carefully to consider the impact of 1992 on Britain and to examine the possibilities of ameliorating its effects. We cannot afford, as on entry to the EEC, to trust blindly to market forces which may well again work to our disadvantage. We should above all, take a positive attitude to cooperation with our European partners to ensure both general economic expansion and also a realistic basis for a British contribution to the economic health of the Community.

As indicated earlier, there are strong arguments for putting sterling fully into the EMS with an ample flexibility margin and at the right rate of exchange which must be well below 3DM to £1. But this should be done only as part of a carefully considered package of our involvement in Europe and of the function of the Community. If we are to move, even slowly, towards a united Europe, it is vital that there is provision for correcting imbalances when one region, one country, or a group of countries begin to fall into the status of depressed areas. If there is no provision for major balancing measures, such a process tends to be strongly cumulative as we have seen only too clearly within our own country. These considerations point strongly in the direction of a much larger Community Budget.

In a unified state, the taxation and budgeting processes naturally tend to correct regional imbalances to some extent e.g. by redistribution from richer people and companies to the poorer areas. This tendency is generally reinforced by specific government policies designed to resurrect depressed regions, inadequate though the resulting measures may be. The European Community operates such policies to some extent. The total of all these influences and measures is already demonstrably inadequate in bringing real life to many areas in Northern Britain for example. So if we are to be exposed to even stronger market forces which will tend to depress further both the UK in general and Northern Britain in particular, there must be much more powerful arrangements in place and much greater resources available to correct the growing imbalances.

Within a few years we face the prospect of:
    – much freer intra European trade from 1992
    – entry into the EMS
as well as pressure for:

- a common European currency
- a European Social Charter
- even the formation of a Central European Bank

Much learned and political debate has recently developed about the extremely complex issues involved in all these developments with their mutual interactions. This is not the place to seek to disentangle all these intertwined strands and to draw a blueprint for the future of Britain in Europe. Some general observations may however be ventured.

In the first place it is wise to be very cautious about rushing into all these supernational systems which will reduce the flexibility of British economic policy and expose us more and more to forces or organisations over which we have little or no control. In this negative respect there is much to be said for current official government policy as well as for the cautious approach of the Labour Party.

On the other hand it is reckless to welcome the freer trade of 1992 on its own and believe this will be beneficial to Britain, against the lessons of history, and to refuse to have anything to do with the other developments favoured by the rest of Europe. For one thing the other Europeans will go ahead any way and we would be well advised to play a full part in discussions to protect our own interests. Secondly, we do need to secure the protection of some of the measures being considered, including some provisions of the Social Charter. It will be essential to secure agreement on general economic policies which will work towards general expansion and enable Britain to increase employment and production. None of these European developments will however rescue Britain unless internally we take the necessary steps to put our own house in order – to revitalise our manufacturing industry, to produce many more of the goods we consume, to increase investment both in industry and in the infrastructure, to raise the standards of general education and especially technical and vocational training to much higher levels and in general to catch up with our European partners and competitors.

To take the contrary view that all that is required is to reduce trade barriers is likely, in the process of denying the lessons of history, to lead to the worst of all worlds. To raise the concept of free markets to the status of unreasoning dogma is to make trade our unbending master rather than our useful servant. The British people have benefited greatly from the development of international trade over the last two centuries, but many of the benefits have been a long time coming and in the meantime many of the people have suffered grievously over long periods. Many are still deprived of a decent and skilled working life and the benefits of educated interests and leisure. The people now have the right to assert that trade should be managed in their interests rather than that they should be managed, or neglected, in the interests of trade for trade's sake.

Appendix I

Education and Training

The new middle classes which developed in the nineteenth century were strongly attracted by the same philosophy of life as the old moneyed classes. If they could not afford to send their children to the so-called public schools, they increasingly had the benefit of the grammar schools which grew strongly during the century and which for the most part tended to ape the classical bias of the public schools. The famous Rugby School owed its original endowment to an Elizabethan merchant called Lawrence Sheriff who had founded a school for the boys and girls of the locality. In Dr Arnold's day – in the first half of the century – there was a continuing battle between the need to accommodate some of the sons of the local merchants, and the financial attractions of providing board and lodgings for the sons of the well-to-do from far and wide. Of girls of course there was no sign at all. Eventually, later in the century, a separate grammar school had to be formed to give effect to the founder's intentions – if only for boys. It was adorned with the inspiring title of 'The Lower School of Lawrence Sheriff'.

For, as R.H. Tawney continually proclaimed in the 1920s and 1930s, English education was organised essentially on a class basis. Before 1870 there had been only a scattered provision for the working classes, essentially on a private basis with some state assistance. By the mid-Victorian period it had become obvious that much more needed to be done. England was clearly falling behind other countries, particularly Germany, in looking after the ordinary people, despite her advanced industrial position and fast accumulating wealth in the hands of the industrialists and commercial people. As the pressure of the humanitarians gradually prevented children being employed in factories, it was necessary to find something else for them to do as an alternative to roaming the streets

143

of the mushrooming cities. Further, the slow extension to the middle and lower classes of the right to vote was inconsistent with their being uneducated, although there were many in the governing classes who feared the effect of the ordinary people knowing too much, a philosophy which found vocal supporters right through the inter-war period of the twentieth century.

So the 1870 Elementary Education Act was passed, providing for the establishment of local school boards to fill in the gaps left by private provision, with powers to pass bye-laws requiring attendance at school of all children aged between 5 and 13. The very mixed pattern of the application of this power forced the government eventually to pass general laws requiring, by 1899, attendance up the the age of 12 at least. Even with this niggardly progress, the levying of school fees was only slowly discontinued until it was finally abolished in 1918.

During this long period when a public elementary education system was being forged, the middle class (or that part of it not wealthy enough to join the upper classes in patronising the public schools) was strengthening its grip on the grammar schools so as to make it very difficult for working-class children to penetrate their preserve. The essentially private system of secondary education was extremely variegated and uneven until the 1902 Education Act introduced a national public system of secondary education.

Even then the system remained very mixed, encompassing the privately-owned grammar schools, which were subjected to a degree of control by new local education authorities, as well as the other secondary schools which they were to take over and to supplement with new County grammar schools. Scholarships were to be provided for able elementary pupils to transfer to secondary grammar schools without paying fees, although the great majority of places would still go to fee-payers. Some provisions were also made for expanding technical education which had so far been sadly neglected, but the basic secondary school was still to be organised on the grammar school basis.

By 1914 only 2½% of each age group in the elementary schools obtained free places in the grammar schools. Even by 1939 the proportion had risen only to 10%, and a fair proportion of this exiguous fraction were the sons and daughters of parents who could afford to pay fees but saved their money by sending their children to the state elementary schools in order that they could win scholarships. If they failed to do this, they went to the grammar schools anyway and their parents paid the fees. The typical annual entry to a grammar school in the 1930s was one third scholarship children paying no fees, one third from the elementary schools paying fees, and one third from private and preparatory schools which were often in junior departments of the grammar schools.

Thus the class system of English education continued right up to the Second World War. Clearly, if only 10% of the elementary school children obtained free places at the grammar schools and some of these had parents who could have afforded to pay fees, probably only some 6 or 7% of working class children attended grammar schools where they were outnumbered by three or four to one by middle class children. The latter only had to pass a modest entry examination to go to the grammar school and very few normal children were excluded although many were 'drop-outs' at the age of fourteen or fifteen.

The most devastating consequence of this social pattern was the enormous waste among the talented working class. A 1938 Study estimated that the total number of children with the ability to benefit from secondary education (arbitarily defined by an I.Q. of at least 130) but who did not have the opportunity to do so was about three times those who did. Virtually none of those gaining free places failed to justify their selection, whereas about half of the fee-paying grammar school pupils failed by the same standard. It follows that, on merit alone, the elementary school children should not only have displaced half of the fee-paying grammar school children but also, if places had been available, could have much more than doubled the total number of successful grammar school pupils. Waste indeed.

The above calculations are based on the I.Q. measure of potential, by a criterion which qualified for secondary education only a quarter of pupils educated at the expense of the state compared with half of the private fee-paying sector, which is an unlikely hypothesis in itself.

It is true that in the inter-war years there was a slow growth in the provision of higher-grade elementary education either in 'Central' schools or in trade and technical schools but those were for limited numbers of pupils and did not begin to compare with the grammar schools in scope or status. They were in fact the precursors of the secondary modern and technical schools established after the Second World War. In education, as in much else to do with social and economic development, it is important to realise the everlasting continuity of things and how slowly the pattern changes. Once the country of England was set on a very slow and class-ridden educational path in the mid-nineteenth century, the very same forces which had fashioned its effective beginning were to remain dominant in channelling its future course.

Even the major Butler Act of 1944 changed less than it appeared to. The abolition of fees for grammar schools, the principle of equal parity for all secondary schools and the raising of the school leaving age to 15, all seemed radical enough. The implication that perhaps half the middle class children, who would otherwise have attended the grammar schools on a fee-paying basis, would have to be content with secondary modern or technical schools, was a threat which was to make the 'passing of the 11 plus' a crucial matter for most middle-class children. For very few parents regarded the alternatives as acceptable, especially as the resources available dramatically to raise the standards of the pre-war non-grammar schools were extremely limited.

So the middle classes spent much money and effort in avoiding the implications of the new system. They increasingly sent their children to private preparatory schools or paid for special coaching to enhance their chances of passing the 11-plus. In any event their children inevitably had better chances than working-class youngsters flowing from the obvious benefits of living in the educated atmosphere of homes created by people who had themselves had the privilege of attending grammar schools. And if, despite all these advantages, a middle class child unexpectedly failed the 11-plus he or she would probably be sent to a private grammar school where (surprise, surprise) he or she would quite likely be successful enough to pass the same examinations at 16 or 18 as the grammar school pupils.

For the validity of selection at 11 years of age, with its crucial consequences, was increasingly called into question. It does not serve the purpose of this present essay to enter into this prolonged debate. It is sufficient to note that many local education authorities were so impressed by the arguments against this continuing division in education and by the need to raise the level for all pupils, that they moved over to the comprehensive system. The London County Council in fact made this decision during the 1939–45 war and proceeded thereafter progressively to implement it although allowing many semi-independent grammar schools to remain for a long time. At the other extreme, some areas still retain in 1989 the 11-plus exam and less advantaged schools for the majority of children who fail it.

It is not necessary for us to become involved in the debate about the degree of success or failure of the comprehensive system except to note that the percentage of children passing O and A levels has steadily risen during the post-war period. It is also true that standards in many of the non-grammar secondary schools were gradually improved and that private education continued to develop and flourish. But the important point is that the comprehensive school was in practice the first really substantial step towards a major demolition of the class basis of education in England.

Even so, it is vital to appreciate the slowness of the change and the durability of the established pattern. For the long history of class division had ensured that only a small minority of working-class children progressed through educational opportunity into the educated middle class. So the vast majority of English children until recently were born into families with no experience or tradition of the kind of education which people who have attended grammar schools take for granted. This great educational class divide is also a major social barrier closely mirrored also in industry and commerce: the shop floor verses the bosses; 'we' and 'they'.

As we have noted above, there have always been voices raised against providing too much working class education because a large proportion of people had inevitably to be content to serve as factory fodder. Quite apart from the social morality of such views, the issue of major concern is that until very recently there has been a gross waste of the talents of bright working-class children who could have more than doubled the ranks of people qualified to take leading roles in society, particularly in industry and commerce.

This waste of potential managerial ability has been the more tragic because it has been compounded by the whole specialised bias of the education of the middle and upper classes especially towards the classics, but also embracing languages and literature, even science to some extent, but with comparative neglect of technology and engineering and particularly of industrial and commercial management. Most im-portant of all, perhaps, is the consideration that the management of people of a different and lower class has been one of the major failures of the middle and upper classes. Indeed the lack of interest of these classes in industrial management has meant that a high proportion of senior positions has been filled by promotion within companies of poorly educated and trained men with narrow horizons.

In the inter-war period the development of the technical schools had been extremely slow, with little encouragement coming from industry which was preoccupied with its own short term problems. By 1938 the number of children in technical schools was a mere 5% of the number in grammar schools. After 1945 change was at first slow but eventually substantial progress was made as part of the general drive for the expansion of Higher Education. The 1956 White Paper on Technical Education led to the designation of ten colleges of Advanced Technology, whilst the 1963 Robbins Report on Higher Education encouraged a vast expansion of the universities with particular emphasis on technological education. With a doubling of university students between 1962 and 1972, science and technology courses particularly benefited.

Eventually there was also a considerable expansion in the development of advanced courses in business and management studies, and belatedly the UK began to catch up with other industrial countries, although the latter have by no means stood still.

Thus on the general educational level the progress since the Second World War has been very considerable, both in the schools and in the colleges and universities, a veritable revolution compared with the earlier decades. Even the yawning gaps in the technological field have been greatly reduced. All this progress is undoubtedly having a gradual effect on the professional quality of industrial management, although the legacy of past amateurism and lack of education still remains very evident.

The tragedy is that just at the time when the higher quality of management has begun to bear considerable fruit, manufacturing industry has once again been faced with severe economic problems which have greatly impaired the opportunities for large scale exploitation of the new professionalism especially in the larger companies. At the same time the financial stringency facing most companies has led them drastically to reduce the internal training of their workforce and of future potential employees. The traditional apprenticeship scheme, in particular, has almost disappeared.

Between 1968 and 1985 the number of apprentices in manufacturing fell from 236,000 to 73,200 and has almost certainly fallen further since 1985. The number of other trainees fell from 209,000 to 39,000 in the same period. In both cases the reductions were particularly severe in the 1980s with a fall of 50% in five years. Clearly short-termism has affected companies in the manufacturing sector to the extent that virtually none of them have felt able to have proper regard to the medium and long term requirements of the country for skilled manpower.

So although the UK showed distinct signs in the post-war period of catching up a little in both general education and technical training, it is still well behind the major industrial countries. With typical thoroughness the Germans established a strong state system of education with a substantial technical content in the nineteenth century and despite losing two world wars, have effectively developed it since to the point where, in the 1980s, the percentage of young people not moving after compulsory schooling to full time education or training, including apprenticeship, is in single figures compared with something nearer to 50% in the UK before the special government schemes adopted recently to alleviate the unemployment situation.

The stark contrast between the UK and Germany in respect of both the general educational level and the extent to which their industrial workers are properly trained, has a major

impact on the efficiency of quite basic industries such as clothing and furniture manufacture, as is demonstrated by the
1987 and 1989 reports quoted in Chapter X. Typically, 80–
90% of German employees have been fully trained on three
year courses, whereas virtually no British employees have
similar training or gain proper qualifications. The inevitable
result is the less effective use of machinery and particularly of
automation. There is a vast gap in productivity. British firms
are confined to low-quality repetitive production of low value,
a field in which, particularly in clothing, they are progressively
exposed to cheap imports from the Far East.

These failings are well beyond the powers of individual
companies, however well-managed, to remedy. They are the
result of a century of neglect of both general and technical
education for working people. Special government schemes
in recent years mainly in the shape of YTS schemes have
begun to scratch at the problem. But as one of the above mentioned reports says, 'We found no evidence that YTS – as
developed so far – would be sufficient to raise workforce
capabilities to German levels'. The other, 1989, report con-
cludes 'We see no evidence that these policies will bring about
an increase of adequate dimension in the breadth of training
that will be required by tomorrow's industry'.

In January 1989 it was reported that the French government was planning to raise the percentage of 18 year olds taking the baccalaureat examination (equivalent approximately
to 'A' levels in the UK but much broader in its scope) from
40% to 80% by the year 2,000. This is a formidable task, but its
significance lies in its even being discussed when one realises
that the starting point for the French is over twice as high as
the present UK position. Anyone who has done substantial
business with French companies will have encountered the
formidable young managers, products of the Grands Ecoles
Polytechniques, who are equally at home in private or public
industry, thus clearly demonstrating the importance of the
quality of management as distinct from ownership. These
people work closely with government departments in a con-
certed effort to achieve results beneficial to both company and
country.

It was Napoleon, with whom we began this essay, who
called the English 'a nation of shop-keepers'. Today he might

be even more derisive. A recent study of training for retailing in France and Britain reported vast differences in standards in the two countries: 'The typical French salesperson is trained in specialised product-knowledge, has been examined in practical selling, and progressed further in general educational subjects (native language, mathematics, a foreign language) as part of his vocational course. Expectations in Britain are lower: little is required for the main corresponding retail training qualifications by way of product-knowledge, and general educational subjects are rarely pursued'.

In the USA the picture is different again but college courses in vocational subjects are wide-spread and over half the population goes from high school to some kind of further education on a substantially full time basis.

It may well be objected that the best of British education is second to none and superior to most. This is undoubtedly true. The trouble is that the pinnacle is too narrow and too specialised right down to the sixth-forms in secondary schools, resulting in the production of many engineers who are only semi-literate and semi-civilised in the humanities, and many literary people who are innumerate. Very few of them are trained in management or even interested in the essential roles of production management and selling.

Lower down the educational pyramid there are still far too many children in poor quality secondary schools who leave in many cases without proper jobs to go to and inevitably to swell the vast ranks of adults whose education has been meagre and who are far less concerned about the quality of education than most people in comparable countries. To cap it all, the valuable old apprenticeship system has virtually disappeared and the general level of technical and vocational training compared with countries like Germany and France is so inadequate as to constitute a major handicap to efficiency and competitiveness for much of British industry.

Appendix II

Unemployment

In earlier chapters we have noted that unemployment became a measurable scourge in the late nineteenth and early twentieth centuries, fluctuating considerably with the trade cycles and sometimes going above 10%. In the inter-war years it became a major blight on the economy and on the people, ranging between 8 and 15% and it was still at 8% of the total workforce in 1938 after substantial economic recovery.

During the first twenty years after 1945, the figures were astonishingly better at no more than 2% but there was some worsening in the late 1960s which was significantly exacerbated by the early deflationary policy of the Heath Government from 1970, almost fulfilling the developing threat of going above one million (or 4%) in 1972 before the politically conscience-stricken expansion of the economy reversed the trend for the time being.

A substantial improvement continued so that the total of workless people was reduced by about a third until the world deflation and British balance of payments problem, induced by the enormous oil price increases, together with consequential governmental measures, finally sent the total above the one million mark in 1975, rising further to a peak of almost one and a half million in 1977, but with a reduction of over 150,000 by 1979.

The major deflationary measures of the Conservative government, described in Chapter X, sent the total rocketing to over two million in 1980 and three million by 1983 and only beginning to improve later in 1986. Over two million jobs were lost between 1979 and 1983 including 1.8 million in manufacturing industry. Between 1983 and 1986, manufacturing jobs had fallen a further 0.3 million, but non-manufacturing increased by nearly a million, a completely unbalanced situation. The total labour force increased by about a million between 1983 and

1986, mainly because of population changes, so unemployment continued to increase slowly. From 1986 onwards the increase in employment outpaced the increase in the labour force so unemployment officially fell by 800,000 by mid 1988. It seems highly likely however that the unemployment total was being artificially reduced. However, by mid 1989 the official total was down to some 1.8 million.

The basis of calculation for the official unemployment figure changed so many times – indeed as many as twenty-eight – between 1979 and 1989 that it is quite impossible accurately to relate the current figure to the 1979 total. One of the most important changes, in 1982, was to restrict the number of people counted as out of work to those successfully claiming state unemployment benefit – the so-called 'Claimant' basis. A recent change has been to exclude people under 18. There can be little doubt that between half a million and a million extra people would be counted as unemployed today if the 1979 rules were still in operation. As we shall see, it is not just a question of the precise terms of the legal rules, but also the methods by which the system is administered.

It was a well known Conservative MP and former Cabinet Minister, Sir Ian Gilmour, who commented that the government seemed to be more concerned with reducing the unemployment figures than with reducing unemployment. It was of course a most astute process which was adopted. If you define the 'unemployed' as being the people who are being paid unemployment benefit and then tighten up the eligibility rules, you obviously kill two birds with one stone – saving money and making the numbers look more respectable.

Anyone who has tried to derive precision and clarity from the unemployment statistics must have felt himself blundering in a quagmire of confusion. At times one begins to suspect the miasma has been deliberately concocted. Of only one proposition can one feel reasonably assured i.e. that by now the government has reduced the official unemployment count to something approaching the minimum figure possible relative to the true position, not only to put the best possible complexion on its economic policy but also simply to save any unnecessary expenditure on benefits.

However, it is worth going into a little more detail of the processes by which unemployment is estimated. There are two

principal methods. First, in the spring of each year a direct survey is made of a large sample of households throughout the
country which produces an estimate of unemployment by
reference to the international (OECD/ILO) definition which
includes the condition of being available for work in the following two weeks. The results of each survey are published in April
of the following year – The Labour Force Survey.

Secondly, a monthly count of the unemployed is made by
reference to the number of claimants for benefit, the test for
which is different from the OECD/ILO definition, partly
through omission of the availability for work criterion.

Now it might well be supposed by the uninitiated that the differences between the results of these two methods ought to be
fairly small. Indeed the totals have come out very close in the last
two years – 2.88 million against 2.95 million in 1987 and 2.37
million against 2.41 million in 1988. Yet the truth is more hidden than revealed by these similarities in the totals. The quite
extraordinary fact, which has attracted surprisingly little comment, is that the actual numbers of people common to the two
totals was no more than 2.0 million in 1987 and 1.6 million in
1988. The balance of nearly 50% more were different people!

The astonishing truth therefore is that some three quarters of
a million people claiming unemployment benefit are not counted as unemployed on the OECD/ILO definition, mainly
because they are either not available for work immediately or
have not recently looked hard enough for it; the Department of
Employment provides a detailed analysis of these people. On
the other hand, there is a broadly similar number of people who
want jobs but have none and who are regarded as unemployed
for the Labour Force Survey, but who are not entitled to benefit
and are therefore not officially counted as unemployed. The
Department of Employment offers little account of these people
except that about half of them are married women looking for
part-time jobs.

One striking aspect of this latter phenomenon is that, despite
the fall of almost one million in the total numbers of unemployed and an increase in the number of employed people of
over 1.4 million between 1986 and 1988, the total number of the
'out of work' people who are not 'unemployed' has changed
comparatively little in the last few years: it was 810,000 in 1986
and still 750,000 in 1988. It is highly likely that many of the men

and women in this category found jobs in these two years, so they must have been replaced either by fresh people deciding to look for jobs as more jobs became available, or by people who were earlier counted as 'unemployed' but have since had their benefits withdrawn or probably a mixture of these two sources. Either way these factors are significant in a true analysis of what has been happening.

In fact the real truth is even more astonishing. The Department of Employment does not normally publish additional information about the answers to questions put to people by the Labour Force Survey but in response to enquiries it has revealed that in the spring of 1988, in addition to the 2.37 million people qualifying as unemployed on the OECD/ILO measure, there was a total of almost two million more who said they would like a job if one were available, even though they were not necessarily looking for one at the moment or, in some cases, were not immediately available for work. Many of these two million were no doubt the same as some of the three quarters of a million claiming unemployment benefit but not qualified as unemployed on the OECD/ILO definition, but the overlap is unlikely to be complete. We therefore reach a grand total of some 4.5 million people in 1988 who would like work if it was reasonably available, although this number has perhaps fallen below 4 million by mid 1989.

It must not be forgotten that in addition to the mid-1989 official unemployment figure of 1.8 millions, there are also over 0.4 millions on 'work-related Government Training Schemes' which were only introduced in 1983 because of high unemployment. Whatever the merits of these schemes, the people involved can hardly be doing 'real' jobs.

One of the most extraordinary aspects of the whole employment picture is that there is no estimate of the real potential workforce which is independent of the collection of the unemployment figures. Any estimate must of course take account of the changing population structure – the numbers and sex of people in different age groups – this 'demographic' factor is common to all labour force estimates.

The other and more uncertain component in the estimates is the activity-rate, i.e. the percentage of people in each age-group (and sex) who are actively interested in work. The activity rate is in large part dependent on the level of unemployment and specifically on whether it is going up or down. The biggest short-term variant in this respect relates to married women interested in part-time jobs. When unemployment increases substantially many such women tend to resign themselves to the lack of suitable jobs and drift into the 'inactive' category, so reducing the workforce. When the economy expands and more jobs are available, many people (not all of them married women) who have temporarily given up the idea of working, are moved to look for jobs again. In the technical employment parlance, they become 'active' again.

However the impact of this phenomenon on the official labour force figures is severely dampened down because these figures are simply the totals of the officially employed and unemployed at different points in time. As we have seen, the official unemployment figures exclude many people who are in fact looking for jobs. Thus the people who are attracted back into the labour force as employment grows are only included in the official labour force figures if they either become employed or qualify as officially unemployed. So the criteria for counting as unemployed significantly affect the size of the official labour force. The tightening of these criteria will tend to reduce the figures. It is significant that the Department of Employment shows a reduction in the total activity rate for men in the 1984–88 period when employment was rising fairly rapidly, which is quite contrary to common sense and the most likely true position – reference is made again to this point below in connection with a more detailed discussion of male unemployment.

The relationship between the number of people in employment and the number officially classified as unemployed is therefore not the simple one of being the two sole components of a fixed or precisely determined total workforce, but is quite complex. In July 1989 the Bank of England published a Discussion Paper entitled 'The relationship between employment and unemployment' which examined developments over the last twenty years. The authors noted a quite new factor dominating the picture in the last three years. They observed that the increase in jobs was mainly in the non-manufacturing sector and involved largely part-time work and the engagement of women. Thus the people taking such jobs would not have been classified as officially unemployed, and the unemployment figures would not be greatly reduced by the availability of these jobs.

Nevertheless in the last few years there has been a sharp fall in unemployment. The authors of the Discussion Paper state that this has been largely due to the introduction of the Restart interviews and stricter availability-for-work tests. 'Thus the "Restart variable" has since early 1986 contributed approximately 0.75 million to the fall in unemployment.' The official reduction in unemployment was some 1.25 million from March 1986 to mid-1988.

Even the number of people in employment is subject to great uncertainty. The 1988 Labour Force Survey, reported in April 1989, produced out of the hat nearly 500,000 extra jobs not reported hitherto. However, in September 1989 the Department of Employment reported that as a result of the results of the May 1987 Census of Employment, they had reduced the estimated number of people in employment by 425,000. It is abundantly clear that it is impossible to put great trust in any particular set of official figures for either employment or unemployment.

However, taking the latest set of government figures available in October 1989, there was a total increase in employment in Great Britain of some 2.3 million (excluding people on work related Government training schemes) between the nadir of March 1983 and March 1989. Of this figure, only 0.66 million were jobs for men i.e. less than 30% compared with 60% of men in the 1983 total of employed people. Further, some 1.36 million, i.e. 60% of the total, were part-time whereas in the 1983 total only 22% were part-time. In fact 0.86 million of the increase were part-time jobs for women. Clearly, a high proportion of the total increase in jobs between 1983 and 1989 were not of the kind likely to reduce the official employment figures.

Putting all these factors together it seems likely that the total number of unemployed according the 1979 criteria is some 50% higher than the mid-1989 official total of 1.8 million, and may well approach 3 million. Perhaps a million more would like work if reasonable jobs were available.

It is worth considering separately the position for men, the number of whom in full time employment (as distinct from self-employment) actually fell by 133,000 over the six-year period from the low point of March 1983. Even including the self-employed, the numbers of full-time male jobs rose by only

370,000. In the same period the increase in the population raised the numbers of 'active' men by almost half a million and some increase in real 'activity rates' must have raised the male labour force still further. Allowing for this, it is difficult to see how the reduction in the male unemployment count of 860,000 could be remotely consistent with the total official increase in male jobs of 660,000 even adding the 220,000 on work-related training schemes. Any real reduction in unemployment was in any event achieved by part-time employment and engagement on government schemes.

The Department of Employment has acknowledged that the coverage of the current unemployment figures is somewhat narrower than in previous years and publishes figures for those years which it affirms to be consistent with current coverage. These figures effectively indicate an overstatement in the old figures of the reduction in male unemployment since 1983 of some 0.25 million. The real overstatement is probably at least double that figure.

According to the latest official figures, over the whole period from 1979 to March 1989, the number of men in full-time employment (as distinct from self-employment) fell by over 1.5 millions while the male labour force was rising by 0.8 millions – a net comparative deficit of 2.3 millions. Even allowing for self-employment, this deficit was still 1.8 millions.

It is also noteworthy that the official unemployment figure for men in mid 1989 is still 7.5% of the male workforce, remembering that the real figure is probably more like 10% – at least by comparison with the figure in previous decades before the rules were modified many times over. So we are not really much better off in this respect than the late 1930s. It is hardly being unduly male chauvinist to believe that the figures for men are somewhat more important than those for women with their high component of part-time jobs for married women.

The position is dramatically thrown into starker relief by viewing it on a regional basis. In May 1989 male unemployment ranged from an official 3.7% in East Anglia and 4.8% in the South East to 11.9% in Scotland, 12.5% in the North of England and 18.8% in Northern Ireland. When one allows for the under-statement of the true positions represented by these figures and the existence in the Northern part of Britain of substantial pockets of even higher proportions of workless, the dire severity of the situation becomes apparent.

The numbers of registered unemployed just on the banks of the Mersey, Tyne, Wear and Tees total around 180,000 people. Official male unemployment rates range from around 14% in Newcastle to 17% and more in Middlesborough and Sunderland, 18% in Hartlepool, almost 20% in Liverpool and 22% in South Tyneside. These are just the worst areas, and there are many more with rates well into double figures even without allowing for the 'official' unemployed.

There are now so many economic barriers between the North and South of Britain, not least in housing costs and availability, that there is no way in which significant numbers of unemployed people from the North can take jobs in the South where labour bottlenecks and inflationary pressures have begun to develop. So one can properly postulate a kingdom divided into two. The Southern half enjoys virtually full employment almost back to the good old days of the 1950s and 1960s and certainly back at least to the 1970s. The Northern half is as badly off for jobs as in the 1930s.

If by some political miracle Britain was suddenly divided into two countries along a line level with North Wales, the new country, North Britain, would have a real male unemployment rate of around 15% – real that is in the sense that at least one sixth more men are available for work if reasonable jobs could be provided. It is hard to believe that the government of North Britain would not try to take very positive steps to do something about this sad waste of human lives and resources.

What most clearly needs to be done is to restore most of the two million jobs lost in the manufacturing sector – a reduction of over 30% since 1979. No doubt a significant part of this reduction represents an increase in productivity, partly because the less efficient firms disappeared altogether. It is difficult to draw precise conclusions about productivity because the composition of manufacturing industry is now very different from the 1979 position and the part which has disappeared was more labour intensive. What is very clear is that the country's general economic situation means that manufacturing production, which in 1988 finally overtook the 1979 level, needs to be raised by at least 20–30% within a few years to secure the balance of payments and provide scope for economic expansion. A 20% increase would imply about one million extra jobs on top of the present 5.1 millions in Britain; a 30% increase would imply about one and a half million new jobs, all assuming no further increase in productivity; in practice some increase would probably be offset by some consequential jobs, mainly in services. Against a true mid-1989 unemployment figure of some three million, this is the measure of the requirement in order to restore full employment and sustain steady economic growth.

Appendix III

Sources of Information

As explained in the introduction, the basic themes relative to the economic history of Britain for the last two centuries have been in my head for some forty years. For a fair part of this time I have been so directly involved in export businesses that I could hardly escape from the facts and theories related to international trade and the associated governmental policies. So in a very real sense this book has been in the process of gestation for a long time. Nevertheless in order to write it, in a period of three months in 1989, it has been necessary to refresh my mind about the facts and to discover whether research has turned up major new information particularly about the nineteenth century.

Compared with the voluminous political literature which has dominated the study of history in this country, surprisingly little has been written about economic history, which in libraries and bookshops is not even recognised as a subject. Until the last war it was extremely difficult for a student to acquire a reasonably broad and informed appreciation of the major developments, particularly in quantitative form, which has brought Britain to where the country had arrived in 1939. At LSE I found myself drawing my own graphs and diagrams of exports, imports, terms of trade and so on based on what figures I could gather from various sources.

Since then a good deal more has been done to record and interpret the quite unique happenings of the last two centuries, but most of the books seem to have been written either for under-graduates, often recapitulating a series of lectures, or for the economics specialists. Nevertheless it has been useful to read a number of these books and to understand the ways in which other people have viewed the past and the recent economic scene. What is quite surprising is that so little has been written for the non-specialist intelligent person who

161

wishes to understand a major aspect of the history of Britain, which is surely at least as important as the political aspect. Inevitably the writing of economic history for the general reader, as indeed of any other kind of history, involves a high level of selection, interpretation and presentation. Any merit attaching to this book is attributable to these factors rather than to any original research or new facts.

The following have been the most useful of the books I have consulted in recent months, in no particular order –

'The Common People 1746 – 1946'
by GDH *Cole* and Raymond *Postgate*. Published by Methuen in London in 1938 with a second edition in 1946. This is one of the few books which really tried to tell how people lived with some explanation of the principle conditioning factors. A valuable book.

'A History of the British People 1086 – 1970'
by Brian *Murphy*, also available in two parts. Published by Longmans, London in 1973.

'The Development of the British Economy 1914 – 50'
by Sidney *Pollard* (who has written a number of other books, all most informative and incisive) 1962.

The Growth of the British Economy 1918 – 1968'
by G.A. *Phillips* & R.T. *Maddock*. Published in 1973 by George Allen & Unwin.

'British Economy of the 19th Century'
by W.W. *Rostow*, published by the Greenwood Press (Oxford) in 1948. This is the first attempt to analyse the long term trends, as well as the business cycles, in the nineteenth century economy. Still just about indispensable. Very interesting on the Great Depression.

'The Economic History of Britain since 1700'
Edited by Roderick *Floud* and Donald *McCloskey*. Published by Cambridge University Press in two parts in 1981. The various chapters are written by different authors from several countries.

'Sterling'
by Douglas *Jay* published by Sidgwick & Jackson (London) in 1985. Very informative on the effects of joining the EEC.

'Essays in Persuasion'
by John Maynard *Keynes*, published for the Royal Econonic Society in 1972 by the MacMillan Press Ltd. This is a collection of Keynes' most important articles. An absolute joy for the cogency of his arguments and the vividness of the language. An eye-opener for anyone who believes there is much that is new in current economic debates.

'A Perspective of Wages and Prices
by Henry *Phelps Brown* and Sheila V. *Hopkins*, published by Methuen & Co. Ltd at the University Press Cambridge in 1981. An invaluable report on seven centuries of the price of consumables compared with builders' wage rates, based on a vast amount of research. The most authoritative evidence on real wages. The book contains other essays including a particularly interesting one on 'The Climacteric of the 1890s' which discusses the reasons for the lower rate of productivity increases at the end of the nineteenth and the beginning of the twentieth centuries.

'Economic Elements in the Pax Brittanica Studies in British Foreign Trade in the 19th century'.
by A.H. *Imlah* published in Cambridge. Massachusetts in 1958. A useful source of trade figures.

'Abstract of British Historical Statistics'.
by B.R. *Mitchell* & Phyllis *Deane*, published by Cambridge University Press in 1962. A vast collection of figures.

'British Agriculture since 1945'
by B.A. *Holderness*, published by Manchester University Press in 1985. This has a few interesting statistics but is a little short on quantitative analysis.

'Agriculture in the United Kingdom 1988' Ministry of Agriculture, Fisheries and Food
published by H.M.S.O. January 1989. This is the successor to

the Annual Review of Agriculture White Paper. It includes valuable information on production of main crops and meat products in recent years compared to the 1977–79 average and relates production to UK consumption figures.

'*Employment in the 1990s*'.
by Robbie *Gilbert*, published by the MacMillan Press Ltd in 1989. An interesting debunking of what have unfortunately become conventional myths, nostrums and complacency. It makes the point, mentioned in Chapter X, that people generally prefer to buy labour-saving equipment rather than services.

'*Britain Can Work*'
by Sir Ian Gilmour, Oxford 1983

'*Uneven Development (Manufacturing – Services) and De-Industrialization in the UK since 1979*
by J.R. *Wells* of the Faculty of Economics, Cambridge, included in 'Restructuring of the U.K. Economy', Ed. Francis Green, published by Harvester Wheatsheaf, 1989. This paper demolishes the idea of a major shift in consumers' expenditure from manufactured goods to services, and shows that British industry's output has just not kept pace with demand.

'*Don & Mandarin*'
Memoirs of Sir Donald *MacDougall* published by John Murray, London, 1987. This is a particularly valuable 'insider's' account of the Second World War and post-war periods.
Also by the same author:-
'*Studies in Political Economy*'. Volumes 1 & 2 published by Mac-Millan in 1975, and
'*Fifty Years on: Some Reflections*', the Seventeenth Keynes Lecture in Economics to the British Academy, December 1988, to be published in the proceedings of the British Academy towards the end of 1989.

Monthly Review of External Trade Statistics
Published by *Dept of Trade and Industry* and especially the

Annual Supplement which includes quarterly figures going back to 1970. The Department also publishes two quarterly analyses of overseas trade in terms of industries – Business Monitors M Q 10 and M Q 12, the latter of which contains figures for import penetration and export sales ratios for manufacturing industry. These figures are available back to 1975.

'*Long – Run Economic Performance in the UK*' in the Oxford Review of Economic Policy Vol. 4 No.1 Spring 1988, included nine articles, many of which are of great interest. One by Mark Thomas discusses the slowdown in the Pre-World War One Economy. Other subjects include 'Technical Education and Economic Decline 1890/1980' and 'British Managers and the British Economy 1870s to the 1980s'.

National Institute Economic Review for November 1987 and May 1989 include the reports on the furniture (1987) and clothing (1989) industries mentioned in Chapter X and the report on the training for retailing mentioned, together with the other reports, in Appendix I.

'*American Trade Adjustment: The Global Impact*' William R *Cline*, Institute for International Economics, Washington DC U.S.A. – March 1989

'*A Return to Trade Surplus? The Impact of Japanese investment on the UK*' 1989. Chris *Dillow,* Nomura Research Institute Europe Ltd

The relationship between employment and unemployment' M.J. *Dicks* & N. *Hatch* Bank of England Discussion Paper July 1989

Unemployment Unit 9 Poland Street London W1V 3DG – an independent organisation – produces regular briefings on unemployment including critical appraisals of official figures.

Education and Training
In addition to references in many of the above publications and particularly the last two, the subject of Education and its history is extensively covered in many more books than Economic History. Two of the most interesting and useful are:-

The Development and Structure of the English Educational System
by Keith *Evans*, published by University of London Press in 1975. This is an excellent factual statement of the main developments.

Equal Opportunity in Education
by Harold *Silver* published by Methuen in 1973. This is a series of articles written over a long period by various authors including R.H. Tawney. It contains the 1938 Study (referred to in Appendix I) by J.L. Gray & Pearl Moshinsky which is a mathematical treatment of educational opportunity.

On the Public School an interesting book is –

'Thomas Arnold'
by T.W. *Bamford* published in 1960 by The Cresset Press. This is a fascinating account of Rugby School in the first half of the nineteenth century, which changed traditional views of Dr Arnold. It contains an account of the battle between the School and those who sought to give effect to the founder's intentions for the education of local children. By the same author is *Rise of the Public Schools* – from 1837 to 1967.

INDEX